Professional Development for
DIFFERENTIATING INSTRUCTION

An ASCD Action Tool

an ASCD Action*TOOL*

Professional Development for
DIFFERENTIATING INSTRUCTION

Cindy A. Strickland

Alexandria, Virginia USA

1703 North Beauregard St.• Alexandria, VA 22311-1714 USA
Phone: 1-800-933-2723 or 1-703-578-9600 • Fax: 1-703-575-5400
Web site: www.ascd.org • E-mail: member@ascd.org
Author guidelines: www.ascd.org/write

Gene R. Carter, *Executive Director*; Nancy Modrak, *Publisher*; Jennifer Barrett, *Content Development*; Mary Beth Nielsen, *Director, Editorial Services*; Christy Sadler, *Project Manager*; Gary Bloom, *Director, Design and Production Services*; Catherine Guyer, *Senior Graphic Designer*; Mike Kalyan, *Production Manager*; Keith Demmons, *Desktop Publishing Specialist*; Kyle Steichen, *Production Specialist*

All Web links in this book are correct as of the publication date below but may have become inactive or otherwise modified since that time. If you notice a deactivated or changed link, please e-mail books@ascd.org with the words "Link Update" in the subject line. In your message, please specify the Web link, the book title, and the page number on which the link appears.

PAPERBACK ISBN: 978-1-4166-0811-0 ASCD Product #109042 n03/09

Quantity discounts for the paperback edition only: 10–49 copies, 10%; 50+ copies, 15%; for 1,000 or more copies, call 1-800-933-2723, ext. 5634, or 1-703-575-5634.

Library of Congress Cataloging-in-Publication Data
Strickland, Cindy A., 1959-
 Professional development for differentiating instruction : an ASCD action tool / Cindy A. Strickland.
  p. cm.
 Includes bibliographical references.
 ISBN 978-1-4166-0811-0 (pbk. : alk. paper)
 1. Teachers—In-service training. 2. Individualized instruction. I. Title.
 LB1731.S735 2009
 370.71'5--dc22
                                                                          2008048561

16 15 14 13 12 11 10 09   2 3 4 5 6 7 8 9 10

Professional Development for
DIFFERENTIATING INSTRUCTION
An ASCD Action Tool

Downloads

Electronic versions of the tools and additional online-only tools are available for download at **www.ascd.org/downloads.**

Enter this unique key to unlock the files:
GB3A7–0BDC7–C9A12

If you have difficulty accessing the files, e-mail webhelp@ascd.org or call 1-800-933-ASCD for assistance.

Acknowledgments

This action tool is dedicated to the teachers and administrators who have worked so hard and so diligently to examine, practice, and promote best practices both in the classroom and for staff development. In particular, thanks to the teachers and administrators of Harrison Central School District in Harrison, New York, each of whom has helped me sharpen my focus, expand my thinking, and refine my own skills in differentiation.

Thanks also go to my husband Rob, whose patience, love, and support sustain me throughout my work, and to our children Amanda and Michael, whose natural instincts and passion for the power of excellent teaching constantly amaze me.

PART ONE

Introduction and Action Tool Overview

What Is High-Quality Professional Development for Differentiating Instruction?

Watching young people grow is fascinating and exciting, and guiding them in this growth is a privilege and joy. The best teachers know both their content area and their students well. They are flexible and responsive to student need, yet sure and steady in their commitment to help their students grow in key knowledge, understanding, and skills. They are passionate about their work and strive to give their best to students every day.

Watching teachers grow is just as fascinating and exciting. Professional development that helps teachers expand and refine their practices over time affects both the individual teachers and the hundreds of students they work with over the course of their careers. Therefore, like their students, teachers should have guidance from educators who understand both their content (best-practices teaching) and their students (staff development participants). Our teachers deserve the very best staff development we can offer—staff development that is flexible and responsive to teacher variance, yet firmly committed to teacher growth.

Unfortunately, to many educators, "high-quality staff development" is something of an oxymoron. The list of complaints about teacher workshop days is long and most often includes

- "Drive-by" workshops
- One-size-fits-all presentations
- "Been there, done that" topics
- Little or no modeling of what is being taught
- Focus on rotating fads
- Lack of follow-up

All of these complaints often lead educators to feel disillusioned, resent staff development days for the time they take away from the classroom and planning, and take an overall attitude of, "If I just close my eyes, this new initiative, too, shall pass."

Professional Development for Differentiating Instruction

Part 1: Introduction and Action Tool Overview   Section 1: What Is High-Quality Professional Development for DI?

Part One

If we seek to break this pattern of thinking in our efforts to help teachers gain—and refine—their knowledge, understanding, and skill with differentiating instruction (DI), we need to consider the following questions:

- What is high-quality staff development?
- Why differentiate staff development?
- What is the relationship between high-quality differentiation and high-quality leadership for differentiation?

What Is High-Quality Staff Development?

Numerous state and federal organizations have developed key principles of high-quality professional development. These include

- The National Staff Development Council (NSDC): www.nsdc.org/standards
- The U.S. Department of Education: www.ed.gov/policy/elsec/leg/esea02/ pg107.html#sec9101
- Goals 2000: www.ed.gov/G2K/bridge.html

Three key ideas emerge from these organizations and will drive our work in *Professional Development for Differentiating Instruction*:

1. High-quality professional development leads teachers to gain and refine knowledge of both content and pedagogy.
2. High-quality professional development reflects best practices in teaching and learning, helping adults with varied interests, learning profiles, and readiness learn to work together and feel part of a community of learners.
3. High-quality professional development has a positive impact on the classroom in terms of both teacher effectiveness and student learning.

By focusing our staff development efforts around these key principles, we hope to provide administrators and teacher leaders with tools to plan for, implement, and reflect on high-quality staff development that introduces, models, and encourages teachers' continuing journeys along the road to more fully differentiated classroom practices.

What Is the Relationship Between High-Quality Differentiation and High-Quality Leadership for Differentiation?

Change can be difficult. Most of us tend to avoid it, especially if our practices have been successful in the past. In *The Limits of Organizational Change*, Herbert Kaufman suggests that change invites us to experience "the humiliation of becoming a raw novice at a new trade

Professional Development for Differentiating Instruction

Part 1: Introduction and Action Tool Overview   Section 1: What Is High-Quality Professional Development for DI?

Part One

after having been a master craftsman at an old one" (1995, p.13). Good leadership for differentiation, therefore, must recognize the difficulties inherent in changing long-standing teaching habits and beliefs while celebrating the successes that happen along the way. In *Leadership for Differentiating Schools and Classrooms*, Carol Ann Tomlinson and Susan Allan (2000) outline nine principles about change in schools and describe how they relate to leadership for differentiation:

- Change is imperative in today's classrooms.
- The focus on school change must be classroom practice.
- For schools to become what they ought to be, we need systemic change.
- Change is difficult, slow, and uncertain.
- Systemic change requires both leadership and administration.
- To change schools, we must change the culture of schools.
- What leaders do speaks with greater force than what they say.
- Change efforts need to link with a wider world.
- Leaders for change have a results-based orientation.

This action tool offers teacher leaders tools to facilitate the change process, reminding them that teachers will be at varied levels of readiness for change and, consequently, for staff development on differentiation. Furthermore, we must consider and respond to teachers' interests and, most particularly, preferred ways of learning if we wish them to accept—and even embrace—change.

Why Differentiate Staff Development?

While there are certainly differences between kindergarteners and practicing teachers that require variations in teaching practices, good teaching is good teaching. Savvy teachers have always incorporated differentiated practices into their teaching repertoires to a certain degree, whether or not they have called those practices by that name. The trick is to refine and add to those practices over time. If good teachers believe in and strive to increase the amount and kind of differentiation that is evident in their classrooms, then staff developers must do no less. In other words, if we are asking teachers to differentiate, then we must differentiate for teachers!

The key principles of high-quality differentiation include establishing a welcoming and safe classroom, ensuring that what is taught (the curriculum) is of the highest quality, maintaining a commitment to ongoing assessment, offering respectful differentiated tasks, and incorporating flexible grouping practices over time (Strickland, 2007). High-quality differentiated staff development must reflect these principles as well.

Professional Development for Differentiating Instruction

Part 1: Introduction and Action Tool Overview   Section 1: What Is High-Quality Professional Development for DI?

Differentiation requires sustained motivation, hard work, and support from an entire school system. Teachers and administrators must recognize that we do not master differentiation in a day, a week, a month, or even a year. Differentiation is a continuing journey toward expertise in teaching. Just as our students start out at different places in their paths to new learning, so do teachers. To do justice to teachers and to the students they serve, we must accept the need and responsibility to help teachers make this journey, offer the training and support needed to successfully change what happens in the traditional classroom, and find the strength to persevere in our efforts to change without being overwhelmed by the urgency and enormity of the task.

If we truly believe that teachers, like the students they teach, have differing learning needs, we must accept the challenge to differentiate professional development systematically and consistently. We can increase the likelihood of this happening by acknowledging teachers' varied readiness levels for new learning, honoring and celebrating their diverse interests, and understanding their unique preferences for how they learn new information and practice new skills.

Organization of This Action Tool

In this action tool, we will learn to practice what we preach. The staff development activities included here will help us:

- Establish a learning environment that is welcoming and respectful of teachers and administrators at all levels of expertise with regard to differentiation;
- Increase teachers' and administrators' knowledge about, understanding of, and skill with differentiated practices;
- Use ongoing assessment to guide staff development;
- Plan respectful differentiated staff development activities; and
- Flexibly and reflectively group teachers for a variety of learning experiences.

Part 2 of *Professional Development for Differentiating Instruction* provides tools for administrators and teacher leaders. In Section 1 of Part 2, leaders reflect on their own and their district's strengths and weaknesses with respect to knowledge about, understanding of, and skill with differentiated instruction. Various tools encourage leaders to examine their own thinking about differentiation and practice responding to teacher questions and concerns about differentiated instruction. Section 2 of Part 2 includes suggested protocols for examining and critiquing individual differentiated tasks, conducting postobservation conferences focused on differentiated practices, and evaluating and supporting overall teacher growth in the ongoing quest to become more responsive to student differences in readiness, interest, and learning profile.

Part 3 of *Professional Development for Differentiating Instruction* provides differentiated tools for leaders to use with teachers before, during, and after DI-focused professional development. In the spirit of modeling differentiation, the tools incorporate variations for teacher interest, learning profile, and readiness differences. Many of the tools also model specific instructional strategies that are useful in the differentiated classroom. In this way, staff development sessions can not only increase teacher knowledge about, understanding of, and skill with content around differentiation but also inform teachers about many of the pedagogical processes that facilitate differentiation.

- Section 1 of Part 3 offers pre-assessments for readiness, interest, and learning profile so that teacher leaders can plan and carry out appropriately differentiated staff development options. These pre-assessments can also serve as models for teachers' own classrooms.

- Section 2 of Part 3 includes tiered (readiness) support for teachers in writing solid KUD goals (what we want students to **Know**, **Understand**, and be able to **Do** as a result of a learning experience).

- Section 3 provides opportunities for teachers to examine, critique, and design ongoing assessments that can help them identify and respond to varied student needs. It also asks teachers to consider ways in which ongoing assessments themselves might be differentiated. Tools in this section are differentiated primarily for interest but also offer learning profile and readiness options.

- Section 4 offers numerous hands-on activities that help teachers define and design their own respectful differentiation. Some of the tools focus on the philosophical as well as the practical, and others have variations designed to appeal to the analytical thinker, the practical thinker, or the creative thinker, offering numerous opportunities for learning profile differentiation. Differentiation for both interest and readiness is also incorporated into many of the tools.

- Section 5 of Part 3 offers teachers the opportunity to examine their own comfort levels with regard to the practice of flexible grouping. Because the amount and kind of flexible grouping that a teacher offers over time is closely related to the teacher's experience with differentiation, this section offers tools for novice, intermediate, and advanced differentiators.

- Section 6 encourages teacher reflection and the sharing of concerns about managing the differentiated classroom. This section also offers specific advice for dealing with the challenges inherent in operating a multitask classroom.

- Section 7 continues to help teachers add to their knowledge base, focusing on many of the tricky questions that teachers, parents, and students ask about differentiation, including what to do about grading. The tools in this section also model the entry points and RAFT (Role, Audience, Format, Topic) strategies.

- Section 8 continues to model differentiation strategies and provides activities to help monitor the progress being made toward both understanding and using differentiated practices.

Electronic Tools and Resources

Interactive versions of the tools and additional online-only tools are available for download. To access these documents, visit www.ascd.org/downloads and enter the key code found on page vi of this book. All files are saved in Adobe Portable Document Format (PDF). The PDF is compatible with both personal computers (PCs) and Macintosh computers. **Note: You must have the Adobe Acrobat Professional software on your machine to save your work.** The main menu will let you navigate through the various sections, and you can print individual tools or sections in their entirety. If you are having difficulties downloading or viewing the files, contact webhelp@ascd.org for assistance, or call 1-800-933-ASCD.

Minimum System Requirements

Program: The most current version of the Adobe Reader software is available for free download at www.adobe.com.

PC: Intel Pentium Processor; Microsoft Windows XP Professional or Home Edition (Service Pack 1 or 2), Windows 2000 (Service Pack 2), Windows XP Tablet PC Edition, Windows Server 2003, or Windows NT (Service Pack 6 or 6a); 128 MB of RAM (256 MB recommended); up to 90 MB of available hard-disk space; Internet Explorer 5.5 (or higher), Netscape 7.1 (or higher), Firefox 1.0, or Mozilla 1.7.

Macintosh: PowerPC G3, G4, or G5 processor, Mac OS X v.10.2.8–10.3; 128 MB of RAM (256 MB recommended); up to 110 MB of available hard-disk space; Safari 1.2.2 browser supported for MAC OS X 10.3 or higher.

Getting Started

Select "Download files." Designate a location on your computer to save the zip file. Choose to open the PDF file with your existing version of Adobe Acrobat Reader, or install the newest version of Adobe Acrobat Reader from www.adobe.com. From the main menu, select a section by clicking on its title. To view a specific tool, open the Bookmarks tab in the left navigation pane and then click on the title of the tool.

Entering and Saving Text

To enter text on the form, position your cursor inside a form field and click. The pointer will change to an I-beam to allow you to enter text. If the pointer changes to a pointing finger, you can select a check box or radio button. Press Enter or Return to create a paragraph return in the field. Press the Tab key or use your mouse to move between fields. To cancel an entry, press the Escape button to restore the previous text or to deselect a field. **Remember, you must have Adobe Acrobat Professional to save your work.**

Printing Tools

To print a single tool, select the tool by clicking on its title via the Bookmarks section and the printer icon, or select File then Print. In the Print Range section, select Current Page to print the page on the screen. To print several tools, enter the page range in the "Pages from" field. If you wish to print all of the tools in the section, select All in the Printer Range section and then click OK.

PART TWO

Tools for Administrators and Staff Development Leaders

Tools for Administrators and Staff Development Leaders

SECTION 1: DIFFERENTIATION ESSENTIALS FOR LEADERS

Evaluating Your District's Readiness for a DI Initiative

ACTION TOOL

Rationale and Purpose

This tool will help you determine the extent to which your school or district leadership currently possesses the skills and background to effectively promote and support differentiation.

Directions

- Begin by asking participants to brainstorm a list of practices that effectively promote and support differentiation. They may work individually, with a partner, or in small groups.
- Distribute the tool, and compare the participants' lists to the indicated competencies in the left column, "Administrators Who Promote and Support Differentiation."
- Direct participants to the middle column, "How We Are Doing Now." Ask them to write down where they think their school leadership currently stands in relation to the listed factors. In the right column, "The Next Steps," ask participants to record next steps to take to improve current leadership practices and capabilities, including accountability measures.
- Discuss the results. Collect participants' completed tools for further study and planning purposes.

Tips and Differentiation Options

- Separate the three main categories (Know and Practice Differentiation, Provide Support, and Understand Change) for evaluation and discussion at different sessions.
- Ask participants to work at tables in groups of 6–9. Alter the directions to read: "Divide up the three main sections of the chart (Know and Practice Differentiation, Provide Support, and Understand Change) so that all are 'covered' at your table. Work with your partner(s) to rate your school or district in each of the bulleted items of your section. Then, share your ratings and your reasoning with others at your table. Work together to come up with an action plan for addressing areas of concern."
- Ask participants to evaluate their own competencies in each area, rather than their school's or district's.

What to Look For

- Honest evaluation of the district's strengths and weaknesses. If participants do not have enough information to evaluate a particular area, suggest they decide how to find out more.
- Realistic steps for improvement. In other words, encourage participants to make the steps doable in a short period of time (a semester or a year, for example) while considering the district or school resources and culture.
- An overall plan for improvement over time that includes accountability measures.

Evaluating Your District's Readiness for a DI Initiative

Activity

Directions:

- Work alone, with a partner, or in a small group.
- Using the chart on the following pages, review the practices of administrators who effectively promote and support differentiation (left column).
- In the middle column, write down how you think your school leadership currently stands in relation to each factor. Rate your school or your district on a scale of 1 ("We haven't really addressed this much.") to 4 ("We've got it covered! Time to help others!").
- In the right column, record specific ideas for improvement.
- Share your ratings with others at your table. Work together to prioritize your next steps and make an action plan to address the issues.

Part Two

Evaluating Your District's Readiness for a DI Initiative

Activity (Cont.)

Administrators Who Promote and Support Differentiation . . .	How We Are Doing Now	The Next Steps
Know and Practice Differentiation • Acknowledge, celebrate, and respond to variations in students' **and** teachers' readiness, interests, and learning profiles. • Have a thorough understanding of what high-quality differentiation is, why it is important, and its nonnegotiables. • Are knowledgeable about a variety of strategies that support differentiated instruction. • Have a solid knowledge of staff's current practices and competencies in differentiated teaching, or seek out that knowledge before and during staff development opportunities to further support teachers' growth in differentiation • Differentiate staff development for teachers with varied interests, learning profiles, and readiness for differentiated practices.		
Provide Support • Establish an atmosphere that encourages teachers to take appropriate risks in their attempts to grow as professionals. • Hold high expectations for all teachers. • Acknowledge and celebrate current practices that support differentiated instruction. • Provide opportunities, support, and resources for continued training in both the theory behind and the practice of differentiation. • Encourage and provide time for teachers to share their successes and frustrations with differentiation along the way.		

Part Two

Evaluating Your District's Readiness for a DI Initiative

Activity (Cont.)

Administrators Who Promote and Support Differentiation . . .	How We Are Doing Now	The Next Steps
Provide Support (Cont.) • Observe, evaluate, and provide feedback concerning teacher growth over time. • Recognize and support the important role that professionals at all levels of a school system play in supporting high-quality differentiated practices. **Understand Change** • Recognize that change is slow, difficult, and uncertain. • Understand the characteristics of effective staff development for adult learners. • Recognize and acknowledge openly that experienced teachers may feel like beginners all over again when trying to implement differentiation—this can make them doubt their competency after years of feeling like they know what they are doing in the classroom! • Establish expectations for growth: all of us must grow in our ability to respond to student differences. That we must change, grow, and differentiate is nonnegotiable; the path that we each may take is negotiable. • Help staff see the connection between differentiation and all other school initiatives so that differentiation is not seen as yet another add-on to the school's programs. • Share results of the move towards more fully implemented differentiation in terms of achievement and student, teacher, and parent satisfaction with the school experience. • Maintain a long-term commitment to change.		

Pre-assessment for Administrators and Staff Developers

Rationale and Purpose

Administrators and staff development leaders may use the information gathered in this pre-assessment to help judge next steps for their own training and to gain insights into training for staff. At the very least, the answers should spark discussion among leaders.

Directions:

- Distribute the tool. Ask participants to work alone to complete the pre-assessment. Point out that you are modeling something that teachers are asked to do in differentiated classrooms (use pre-assessments). Good staff developers practice what they preach.
- Collect the completed pre-assessments, and use the results to plan further training for administrators and teacher leaders.

Differentiation Option

If you prefer, you may ask participants to complete the pre-assessment in small groups or as a whole group. **Note:** If you need information about individuals' background knowledge in differentiation, ask participants to complete the pre-assessment on their own. If the primary use is to reactivate participants' prior knowledge or start a discussion, then a group pre-assessment is appropriate. In the latter case, distribute a piece of chart paper to each small group, and have them reproduce the diagram in Part 1 on the paper. They may use the back or a second sheet to respond to the questions in Parts 2, 3, and 4.

What to Look For

- See provided samples that represent varied levels of expertise with differentiation. Watch out for misconceptions about differentiation, as well as the degree to which participants see both the details and the overall philosophy of differentiated instruction.
- In Parts 2 and 3, notice that the sentence starter encourages participants to identify the "big ideas," or essential understandings, of differentiation. Look to see if teachers write something like, "Teachers must understand pre-assessment" (a common mistake when identifying big ideas and a sign that they need more help in writing essential understandings) or if they are more specific, writing sentences like, "Teachers must understand that pre-assessment should drive the instruction that follows."
- Part 4 will give you information about the stumbling blocks participants may experience that can impede success and indicate areas for further individual coaching or group work.

Pre-assessment for Administrators and Staff Developers

Sample 1: Novice Level

Part 1: Complete the chart to show what you know about differentiation. Write as much as you can. You may also use symbols or pictures to communicate your thoughts.

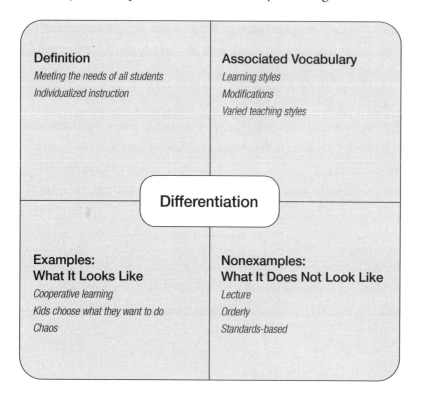

Definition
Meeting the needs of all students
Individualized instruction

Associated Vocabulary
Learning styles
Modifications
Varied teaching styles

Differentiation

Examples:
What It Looks Like
Cooperative learning
Kids choose what they want to do
Chaos

Nonexamples:
What It Does Not Look Like
Lecture
Orderly
Standards-based

Part 2: What are the three most important things to understand about teaching in a differentiated classroom?

1. *Good teachers already do this*
2. *???*
3. *???*

Part 3: What are the three most important things for administrators to understand about leading for differentiated instruction?

1. *Some teachers will resist.*
2. *Some teachers already do this.*
3. *Teachers need more time to plan.*

Pre-assessment for Administrators and Staff Developers

Sample 1: Novice Level (Cont.)

Part 4: What is something that you struggle with when thinking about differentiation or a question you still have?

Seeing the difference between differentiation and cooperative learning.

Pre-assessment for Administrators and Staff Developers

Sample 2: Intermediate Level

Part 1: Complete the chart to show what you know about differentiation. Write as much as you can. You may also use symbols or pictures to communicate your thoughts.

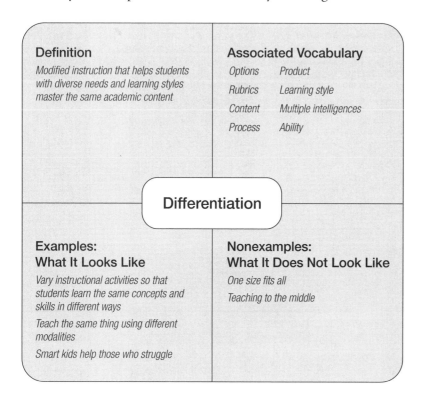

Definition
Modified instruction that helps students with diverse needs and learning styles master the same academic content

Associated Vocabulary
Options   Product
Rubrics   Learning style
Content   Multiple intelligences
Process   Ability

Differentiation

Examples:
What It Looks Like
Vary instructional activities so that students learn the same concepts and skills in different ways
Teach the same thing using different modalities
Smart kids help those who struggle

Nonexamples:
What It Does Not Look Like
One size fits all
Teaching to the middle

Part 2: What are the three most important things to understand about teaching in a differentiated classroom?

1. *Different kids need different teaching.*
2. *Everybody needs to meet or exceed standards, even if they get there in different ways.*
3. *Kids have to be comfortable in the classroom for this to work.*

Part 3: What are the three most important things for administrators to understand about leading for differentiated instruction?

1. *Learning to differentiate is hard work and takes time.*
2. *Different teachers are at different levels with regard to differentiation.*
3. *They need to provide resources to help teachers. Teachers can't do it on their own.*

Pre-assessment for Administrators and Staff Developers

Sample 2: Intermediate Level (Cont.)

Part 4: What is something that you struggle with when thinking about differentiation or a question you still have?

Trying to get teachers to see the value and importance of differentiated instruction for the students and not just as another district initiative

Pre-assessment for Administrators and Staff Developers

Sample 3: Advanced Level

Part 1: Complete the chart to show what you know about differentiation. Write as much as you can. You may also use symbols or pictures to communicate your thoughts.

Definition

Differentiation begins with high-quality curriculum and instruction that are designed to respond as often as possible to the varied interests, learning profiles, and readiness needs of students.

Associated Vocabulary

Interest, learning profile, readiness, learning styles, multiple intelligences, content, process, product, affect, community, Gardner, Sternberg, contracts, RAFT, compacting, ThinkDots, tiered lessons, learning centers or stations, flexible grouping, pre-assessment, KUD.

Differentiation

Examples:
What It Looks Like

Student-centered classroom

A balanced variety of grouping practices and instructional strategies

Students who can self-manage and work both alone and with others

Caring and comfortable environment

Ongoing assessment that impacts follow-up instruction

Respectful activities for all students

Common learning goals

Nonexamples:
What It Does Not Look Like

Teacher-centered classroom: "I teach; you learn."

Some students working on "fluffy" or "dumbed-down" work

Some students always doing more or less work than others

Different learning goals or standards for some students.

Cutthroat competition to be the "best"

Overemphasis on any one instructional strategy (e.g., lecture)

Part 2: What are the three most important things to understand about teaching in a differentiated classroom?

1. *Teachers must understand that they need to vary materials, activities, and assessments and combine them with high-quality curriculum, high-quality instruction, and research-based strategies.*

2. *Teachers must understand that differentiated instruction is not a dumbing down of the curriculum. All students work to key standards.*

3. *Teachers must understand that students learn differently and differentiated instruction facilitates learning and academic growth in all students.*

Part Two

Pre-assessment for Administrators and Staff Developers

Sample 3: Advanced Level (Cont.)

Part 3: What are the three most important things for administrators to understand about leading for differentiated instruction?

1. *Administrators must understand that they need to help teachers to understand the importance of differentiated learning so as to ensure the success of all students. This is done through professional development.*

2. *Administrators must understand that it takes time for teachers to change their belief systems and modify their ways of teaching and that they have to be supportive.*

3. *Administrators must understand that differentiated instruction has a philosophy and classroom implications that the administrator must believe in to support teachers' work.*

Part 4: What is something that you struggle with when thinking about differentiation or a question you still have?

Balancing the need to praise teachers for classroom practices that "fit" the philosophy of differentiation along with the imperative to refine and add to those practices.

Pre-assessment for Administrators and Staff Developers

Activity

Part 1: Complete the chart to show what you know about differentiation. Write as much as you can. You may also use symbols or pictures to communicate your thoughts.

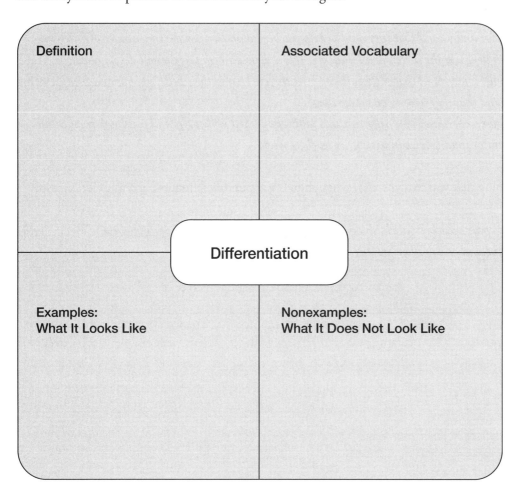

Part 2: What are the three most important things to understand about teaching in a differentiated classroom?

1. Teachers must understand that _____.

2. Teachers must understand that _____.

3. Teachers must understand that _____.

Pre-assessment for Administrators and Staff Developers

Activity (Cont.)

Part 3: What are the three most important things for administrators to understand about leading for differentiated instruction?

    1. Administrators must understand that _____.

    2. Administrators must understand that _____.

    3. Administrators must understand that _____.

Part 4: What is something that you struggle with when thinking about differentiation or a question you still have?

Thinking About Leading for Differentiation

ACTION TOOL

Rationale and Purpose:

This tool models a variation on the cubing strategy, in which participants are asked to roll a cube to determine the task they will do. Each side of the cube has a different question or set of instructions. This variation, called ThinkDots by its creator, Kay Brimijoin, associate professor of education at Sweet Briar College in Sweet Briar, Virginia, accomplishes the same objectives in a slightly different format. Individual prompts are written on cards, and each card has a different number on it. Instead of rolling a cube, students roll a die to determine which numbered task they complete.

This activity works well in starting a discussion about differentiation in general and, more specifically, how administrators might support an initiative in differentiated instruction. It also works well as a closing activity.

Directions

Before the session:

- Make copies of the ThinkDots prompts that are provided. You will need one copy for every 3–6 participants.
- Working with one sheet at a time, cut the ThinkDots squares apart, punch a hole in the upper left corner of each card, and thread the cards onto a key ring or staple them together at the side.

During the session:

- Place administrators in groups of 3–6. Distribute one set of cards and a die to each group.
- Distribute the tool, which contains directions for the participants. Point out that the prompts require complete, thoughtful, and insightful answers, not surface ones.
- Provide index cards for the individual response part of this activity. Collect them as exit cards.
- After participants have completed the activity, discuss how and why it was differentiated. Remind participants of the importance of modeling differentiation strategies throughout the staff development process.

Tips and Differentiation Options

- Use card stock or laminate the cards for durability.
- Groups of 3–4 seem to work best for this activity.
- You can have administrators complete this activity alone in written format. In that case, the roll of the die indicates the order in which they respond to the questions.
- Administrators may also post these questions on a blog to spark discussion about differentiation.
- You may wish to allow participants to pass one time or roll again if they do not feel comfortable answering a particular prompt.

- Use the information from the exit cards to help you evaluate participants' knowledge and understanding of differentiation. You may wish to start a follow-up staff development session with excerpts from these cards.
- You could differentiate Part 1 by changing the question set or the method of responding to the questions based on knowledge of participants' particular interests, learning profiles, or readiness levels.

What to Look For

- Circulate while administrators complete the activity. Jot down particularly insightful thoughts you hear to share in follow-up discussions. Listen also for misconceptions and inaccuracies that need to be addressed.
- In Part 1, all participants use the same set of questions, but they have a choice for each prompt. Part 2 is differentiated according to interest and learning profile. (Some questions are more analytical in nature, some more practical, and some more creative.)

Thinking About Leading for Differentiation

ThinkDots Prompts

1. Evaluate It Talk about a successfully differentiated lesson that you have seen. What made it work? What would you encourage the teacher to try next? OR Talk about a "differentiated" lesson that you observed that, in your opinion, was not really differentiated. What changes would need to be made for the lesson to be truly differentiated?	**2. Analyze It** What is **your own** next step for growth with regard to differentiation? How will you go about taking this step? Be specific. OR What is your school's greatest need when it comes to learning about differentiation? How can **you** help? Be specific.
3. Describe It What does differentiation look like, sound like, feel like? Describe it from the perspective of **one** of the following: Teacher OR Student OR Parent	**4. Apply It** A teacher comes to you who wants to start differentiating her instruction. How would you suggest she begin? OR A teacher comes to you who refuses to be "suckered into yet another fad." What would you say or do to convince her of the merits of differentiation?
5. Argue For or Against It Should a school **require** teachers to differentiate instruction? Explain your reasoning. OR To what extent should differentiated instruction be a part of the teacher evaluation process? Explain your thinking.	**6. Compare It** Compare differentiated instruction to more "traditional" instruction. OR Compare the differentiated instruction model to another model of instruction you are familiar with (e.g., Understanding by Design, What Works in Schools).

Thinking About Leading for Differentiation
Activity Directions

Part 1: Working in groups of 3–6, complete the following activity.
- The first person rolls the die. Whatever number lands on top tells the person which of the numbered prompts to answer. That person should answer the prompt, working for a complete, thoughtful, and insightful answer.
- Next, other group members may add their own thoughts about the prompt.
- The second person rolls the cube. If she rolls a number corresponding to a different prompt, the group should answer it; if the group has already answered that prompt, she should roll again.
- Stop once you have answered all the prompts.

Part 2: Working alone, choose any **one** of the prompts, and write a brief response on the index card provided.

How Would You Respond? Role-Play (Intermediate-to-Advanced)

ACTION TOOL

Rationale and Purpose

Use this tool to help experienced administrators and staff development leaders practice responding to common teacher concerns and thoughts about differentiation. (If participants are new to the coaching process or to differentiation, use the How Would You Respond? Fishbowl tool on page 40.)

Directions

- Paste each provided comment on a separate index card. Distribute them at random. Have participants work in pairs.
- Tell partners that they will take turns playing the role of a teacher discussing differentiation with an administrator.
- The "teacher" should read the comment on his card aloud to his partner. The "administrator" will then have several minutes to respond to the comment. Partners should then switch roles.
- Distribute new comment cards or have teachers switch with another pair, and repeat the process as many times as practical.
- Debrief by asking participants to share their responses to the reflection questions.

Tips and Differentiation Options

- If you make multiple sets of the comments, use different-colored index cards for each set.
- You do not have to use all of the comments. Pick those that most closely match your district's or participants' needs.
- If your participants are particularly comfortable with one another, you may elect to have several role-plays happen one at a time in front of the large group. Solicit additional possible responses to each situation from the audience after they have viewed the role-play.
- As participants work, roam around the room to listen for particularly insightful remarks. Share these with the large group.
- Use the comments as a catalyst for discussion about why staff development for differentiation must be differentiated.
- If you have previously discussed Hedrick's Ascending Intellectual Demand: Differentiation rubric (p. 53), ask participants to share the level of expertise the teacher's comments seem to reveal.

What to Look For

- It is important for administrators to acknowledge teachers' fears and worries. Listen for answers that both appropriately affirm the teachers' comments and push them ahead in their knowledge, understanding, and skill with regard to differentiation—even if they are already quite advanced.
- Teachers' comments can be very revealing about their philosophy of teaching and learning, as well as their current knowledge about, skill with, and understanding of differentiation. Administrators and staff development leaders must be on the lookout for teachers' misconceptions about differentiation and gently correct them.

Part Two

How Would You Respond? Role-Play

Comment Cards

I'm a strong believer in: I teach, I give the examples and generally, by and large, they still have a lot of reading and math to do from their books. Usually that is going back and reading into another facet of what I've already taught. In other words, I'm asking them to make a connection, rather than teach themselves. . . . I believe the students have to be taught skills before they use them.

I feel that I'm in a dichotomy or paradox within my own self a lot of times because I often have to battle with myself on this a lot. I often want it quiet. But I realize that to differentiate well, it's not going to be quiet and so it's like I battle with myself over this all the time because if the learning was taking place and I knew that it was, then I could feel good about it being noisy. But I find often that just more distraction is happening than learning.

I let the students choose. There were some options that were easier than others and of course I didn't have the top five students go right for the harder situation. They chose the easiest. That was one thing I didn't like.

How Would You Respond? Role-Play

Comment Cards (Cont.)

We've got very vocal parents around here. They would not like their child not to get a 99 if they saw someone else getting a 99 for work and their child is having harder work—what they consider hard work—it's hard to explain. But the barriers, I think, are the grading barriers, and until we change the way that students are graded and do it more on "this is where you are, and this is how much you grew during the grading time" instead of giving As and Bs or 60s and 70s, I think that's the biggest barrier [to differentiation].

I am definitely driven by the curriculum guide—I am driven by the state testing and requirements and it's not that I've never used those before, I did. But I felt that I could pace things—I could give students more time to delve—and that type of thing and we could really—we could have more time to do enriching things without feeling like, oh gosh, I've got to move on, I can't stop for this—and this year I definitely do feel very—I feel very—I feel very frustrated—I feel very bound by different things. I just don't feel like they're having the opportunity to really get a good grip on things before I have to move on—and I'm not—I don't assess everything by test, I have a variety of assessments—but unfortunately it's the research type of assessments I like to use and so forth that are getting curtailed.

I looked at some quiz results . . . or their last class work or lab activity and made groupings according to which level, you know, I thought they could achieve at. Um . . . and I think there was one group that was weak and that I probably could have made a couple of switches of stronger children, um . . . or should I say somebody who had a little more leadership.

How Would You Respond? Role-Play

Comment Cards (Cont.)

I had always felt that I know I'm really missing something. I know I'm just not hitting for this child. I always felt successful, but like I never really reached it all and differentiation is—I don't feel like I have really reached it all but this is helping me make certain that the child that was so bright I thought I was losing and the child that was handicapped that never got there—it's helping me think a lot more and it's certainly given me great ideas on how to incorporate things for both types of students. It's something that I know I'm going to be working on over the years and I feel like I've started. I feel a lot better about that aspect of my teaching because of it.

Sometimes, I will scratch my head and I don't even know where to start. I just worry about myself and my cat and just finding time to go to the grocery store. I wonder, what am I doing with my time? Am I not managing my time right? Why am I tired all the time? I feel like I am just going to explode.

How I determined my groups, red, white, and blue—it was, red was the ones I knew had exceedingly high thinking skills and could take some difficult reading matters. Some of them struggled with it . . . some of them soared with it and a few of them still struggled, but that was okay. Then my white group was I guess what you would call the lower group, the ones who have trouble keeping a pace, keeping up with following directions and those types of things. So I tried to differentiate a lot in the way their directions were and how they had to do things. Then my blue group, I guess is what you would call the middle group. . . . I made sure that each group had one artistic assignment.

Part Two

How Would You Respond? Role-Play

Comment Cards (Cont.)

Sometimes you feel a little stressed trying to make sure you do get it all in—but [differentiation] is important enough to me. I feel its importance. It's something I want to do well as a teacher, it's a goal for me. But I'm the kind of person, I can set that goal, but I can also let it unfold over a period of time. I don't necessarily have to be perfect at it today, but I'd like to be perfect at it in about five years.

I would say that I am a good way on the road [of differentiation], but a roadblock has definitely been put up. When I say a roadblock . . . with the amount and the difficulty of the standards I must cover, I have to be sure that every student has actually heard and dealt with everything independently and I can't depend on that with a lot of independent work. The amount of time involved with taking a concept and creating a whole unit with it, I am not talking about my planning time, I'm talking about the class time itself. I no longer have any to spare.

I've been teaching, this is my 25th year and back when I started . . . cooperative grouping was not taught. We just didn't do that. Everybody was in rows and we sat and did our work and although I've learned to teach different things, it has been really hard for me to switch over and teach differently. I know it is like teaching an old dog new tricks and I know that the kids need this.

How Would You Respond? Role-Play

Comment Cards (Cont.)

> Normally with those [high-ability] kids, I know who they are, but I don't do anything different because I try to mix up the groups so I don't have all the high ability kids in one particular group in hopes that the ones with the lower ability will rise to the occasion.

> [Differentiation] really means more effectively meeting the needs of individual students . . . it's a very challenging way to teach, but I think if we meet the students' needs we have to be challenged . . . but it is more rewarding for the students and therefore for the teacher to try and teach that way. . . . The benefits to students are clear. Differentiation is a way of designing instruction to meet the students' need for growth. If students don't show growth, then everybody has been wasting their time.

> My biggest challenge is classroom management and the low skills kids have. They don't do homework. They don't study for tests. I've worked so hard on classroom management and getting them to behave like young ladies and gentlemen, that maybe now we'll be able to get to the teaching.

Source: Adapted from *The Feasibility of High-End Learning in a Diverse Middle School* (pp. 208–283), by C. M. Brighton, H. L. Hertberg, T. R. Moon, C. A. Tomlinson, & C. M. Callahan, 2005, Storrs, CT: National Research Center on the Gifted and Talented, University of Connecticut. The work reported herein was supported under the Education Research and Development Centers Program, PR/Award Number R206R000001; as administered by the Institute of Education Sciences, U. S. Department of Education. The findings and opinions expresses in this report do not reflect the position or policies of the Institute of Education Sciences of the U.S. Department of Education. This document has been reproduced with the permission of the National Research Center on the Gifted and Talented.

Part Two

How Would You Respond? Role-Play

Activity

Directions:

- You and a partner will take turns playing the role of a teacher and administrator discussing differentiation.
- "Teachers" read the comments on their cards aloud to their partners. "Administrators" will then have several minutes to respond to the comments.
- Switch roles and discuss the same comment, or exchange comment cards with another pair and repeat the exercise.
- Discuss and respond to the reflection questions below.

How did seeing these situations from a different perspective help you better determine how to address them?

How can we promote better communication between teachers and administrators about concerns regarding differentiation?

What conclusions can we come to about the best way to respond to teacher comments about differentiation?

How Would You Respond? Fishbowl (Novice)

ACTION TOOL

Rationale and Purpose

Use this tool to help administrators and staff development leaders practice responding to common teacher concerns and thoughts about differentiation. (If participants are experienced with the coaching process or differentiation, you may use the How Would You Respond? Role-Play tool on page 32.)

Directions

- Paste each comment from the How Would You Respond? Role-Play tool (p. 32) onto a separate index card, and distribute them at random. Ask participants to read their assigned comment and spend a few minutes thinking about what the comment reveals about the speaker's beliefs and concerns about differentiated instruction. They should also think about ways that a savvy administrator might respond to the comment to both affirm the teacher's concerns and gently move that teacher forward in her thinking.

- Ask for three volunteers to form a small inner circle in the center of the room. They will be the "fish" in this fishbowl activity. All other participants, including the leader of this activity, should sit in a larger outer circle (the fishbowl).

- One of the three volunteers will play the role of the teacher. The second volunteer will play the role of administrator responding to the comment. The third volunteer will act as observer or coach to the administrator.

- Encourage the "teacher" and "administrator" to engage in a conversation lasting 2–3 minutes. The "teacher" should begin by reading aloud the comment on his or her assigned card. The "administrator" should respond to the comment and to any underlying concerns about differentiation that the comment or the ensuing conversation seems to reveal. At the conclusion of the role-play, ask the observer to comment on the efficacy of the teacher–administrator conversation.

- When the small-group discussion begins to dry up, ask the larger circle, the "fishbowl," to add their thoughts. Ask the "fish" to switch roles or repeat the exercise with a new set of volunteers.

- At the end of the session, debrief by asking participants to share their responses to the discussion question.

Tips and Differentiation Options

- If you make multiple sets of the comments, use different-colored index cards for each set.

- You do not have to use all of the comments. Pick those that most match your district's or participants' needs.

- Use the comments as catalyst for discussion about why staff development for differentiation must be differentiated.

- If you have previously discussed Hedrick's Ascending Intellectual Demand: Differentiation rubric (p. 53), ask participants to share the level of expertise each teacher's comments seems to reveal.

What to Look For

- It is important for administrators to acknowledge teachers' fears and worries. Listen for answers that both appropriately affirm the teachers' comments and push them ahead in their knowledge, understanding, and skill with regard to differentiation—even if they are already quite advanced!
- Teachers' comments can be very revealing about their philosophy of teaching and learning, as well as their current knowledge about, skill with, and understanding of differentiation. Administrators and staff development leaders must be on the lookout for teachers' misconceptions about differentiation and gently correct them.

Part Two

41

How Would You Respond? Fishbowl

Activity

Directions:

To prepare for the fishbowl:

- Read your assigned teacher comment and spend a few minutes thinking about what the comment reveals about the speaker's beliefs and concerns with regard to differentiated instruction. You may want to jot down your ideas.
- Think about ways that a savvy administrator might respond to the comment to both affirm the teacher's concerns and gently move that teacher forward in his or her thinking. You may want to jot down your ideas.

During the fishbowl:

- If you are a "fish," you will be assigned one of three roles: teacher, administrator, or observer.
  - If you are the teacher, begin a conversation with the administrator by reading the comment on your assigned card. Think about what the comment reveals about the speaker's beliefs and concerns to make your conversation as realistic as possible. Continue the conversation for 2–3 minutes.
  - If you are the administrator, respond to the teacher's comment and to any underlying concerns about differentiation that the comment or the ensuing conversation seems to reveal. Your job is to acknowledge the teacher's thoughts and concerns and to move that teacher forward in his or her thinking about differentiation.
  - If you are an observer, play close attention to the conversation, and be ready to make recommendations about other ways in which the administrator might both affirm the teacher and push ahead his or her thinking about differentiation.
- If you are a part of the "fishbowl," you will be asked to add your own thoughts on the conversation and to draw conclusions about effective ways to respond to teacher comments about differentiation.

After the fishbowl:

Respond to the discussion questions on the next page.

How Would You Respond? Fishbowl

Activity (Cont.)

How did seeing these situations from a different perspective help you better determine how to address them?

How can we promote better communication between teachers and administrators about concerns regarding differentiation?

What conclusions can we come to about the best way to respond to teacher comments about differentiation?

Tools for Administrators and Staff Development Leaders

SECTION 2: EVALUATING DIFFERENTIATION

What to Look For When Evaluating Differentiated Activities

ACTION TOOL

Rationale and Purpose

Use this tool to help you evaluate differentiated activities developed by your staff (or by other sources).

Directions

Distribute copies of the tool to administrators and staff development leaders. Instruct them to use the questions as a guideline when evaluating differentiated lesson plans from their staff.

Tips and Differentiation Options

- Questions 1–3 may be used with or without classroom observation or follow-up discussion with the teacher.
- The first three questions are also helpful when teachers are evaluating their own or their peers' work.
- Questions 4–7 are appropriate for classroom observation and debriefing conferences.
- Leaders may prefer to focus on specific questions when using the protocol, depending on what teachers have been working on. For example, if your staff development focus has been on KUD goals, then evaluate the examples primarily for that aspect.
- To use this tool as a learning activity for administrators and staff development leaders, distribute a common sample differentiated activity along with the tool. After individuals or pairs of leaders have used the tool to evaluate the work, compare your responses.

What to Look For

- Question 1: Look for curriculum that is relevant, engaging, and standards-based. Watch out for activities that appear to be time fillers or that take more time than their overall importance seems to merit.
- Question 2: Respectful activities are equally engaging and challenging. Every version leads to the same or very similar goals. In particular, the versions should lead to the same understanding.
- Question 3: Every version—even the most basic—should challenge the students for whom they are designed. Watch out for artificially low ceilings. Be sure that the most advanced versions also have appropriate scaffolding when necessary.
- Question 4: An activity can usually be differentiated in multiple ways. The type of differentiation teachers choose is less important than their ability to explain the rationale behind their decisions.
- Question 5: High-quality differentiation relies on data—qualitative and quantitative, formal and informal. To what extent has the teacher ensured a purposeful match between student and activity?

Part Two

- Question 6: This question can usually be answered only after examination of multiple instances of differentiation.
- Question 7: To what extent do students notice the differentiation? Do they seem to be bothered by different students doing different activities?

What to Look For When Evaluating Differentiated Activities

Activity

Use the following questions to help you evaluate differentiated examples from your staff.

Question	Evaluation
Is this good curriculum? Is it worthy of teacher and student time?	
Do the differentiated tasks seem equally respectful? Does each task appear to lead to the same goals (KUD)?	
Do all versions of the task require students to stretch as much as possible?	
What type of differentiation does this illustrate (readiness, interest, or learning profile)? Was this a good choice, given the goals and the students for whom the activities were designed?	
What kind of assessment data was used to decide (a) the type of differentiation; and (b) who would do which task? How appropriate was this data? Did it help improve the match between task and student?	
Is this the only type of differentiation you ever see this teacher using? If so, is that appropriate, or is the teacher stuck in a differentiation rut?	
How do students appear to feel about differentiation?	

Part Two

Debriefing with Teachers

ACTION TOOL

Rationale and Purpose

Use this tool as a discussion guide for debriefing sessions with teachers.

Directions

Distribute copies of the tool to administrators and staff development leaders. Instruct them to use the questions when conducting debriefing or coaching sessions following observations. Remind them that for differentiation to remain a district or school focus, teacher feedback should always include a discussion of differentiated practices.

Tips and Differentiation Options

- You do not have to use all the questions or ask them in a particular order.
- Teachers could answer these questions as part of a written summary that they complete prior to a postobservation conference.

What to Look For

People can think about and plan for differentiation in multiple ways. Watch for misconceptions and misapplications, but focus mainly on whether or not teachers are thinking carefully about what they plan and reflecting thoughtfully on the outcomes of their plans.

Debriefing with Teachers

Activity

When talking to a teacher about a differentiated activity or lesson, choose from the following questions. Use the chart below to record notes about your discussion with the teacher and how you might follow up.

Teacher name: _____

Questions	Teacher Responses	My Thoughts/Follow-up
What were your objectives for this activity?		
Why did you feel the need to differentiate this activity?		
How did you decide the kind of differentiation to use (readiness, interest, learning profile)? In retrospect, was this a good choice? Why?		
How did you decide who got which version? Did you make the right choices? Explain your thinking.		
Did you tell students that the activity was differentiated? Why or why not? Was this a good choice? Why or why not?		
How did you handle the management issues—giving multiple directions, rearranging the room, distributing materials, dealing with early finishers, and so forth?		
What other changes to the activity would you make if you could do it again?		

A Differentiation Rubric:
Planning for Teacher Growth

ACTION TOOL

Rationale and Purpose

This tool provides a detailed rubric of a teacher's journey from novice to expert in differentiation, along with suggestions on what teachers at each level need to move to the next level of competency. Use this tool to help you identify where your teachers are with respect to knowledge about, understanding of, and skill with differentiation and to help you set differentiated staff development goals for individuals or small groups of teachers.

Directions

- Distribute the tool and the rubric. Ask administrators and staff development leaders to use the tool to help them identify their own level of expertise with respect to differentiation.
- Examine the "What Does the Learner Need at Each Stage?" rubric to help participants identify a variety of ways to support educators at varied stages of expertise. Solicit additional suggestions from participants for supporting educators.
- Ask participants to complete the provided chart for teachers they work with who (if possible) have different levels of differentiation expertise.
- Ask participants to share their thoughts about and plans for helping teachers at different skill levels. If appropriate, use the results to assign teachers to specific follow-up staff development activities.

Tips and Differentiation Options

- This rubric may also be used as a self-assessment and goal-setting tool by teachers.
- As you look at the descriptors, remember that it's not unusual for a teacher's skills to overlap from one column to the next.
- Consider asking administrators and staff development leaders to devise their own rubric descriptors or adapt Hedrick's rubric to better match the district's focus and philosophy.

What to Look For

- Thoughtful consideration of teacher level of expertise based on specific observations rather than just general impressions
- Appropriate match between teacher level of expertise and next steps for growth

A Differentiation Rubric: Planning for Teacher Growth

Ascending Intellectual Demand: Differentiation

Novice	Apprentice	Practitioner	Expert
• Unsettled by the ambiguous and organic nature of differentiation. • Seeks algorithmic processes and expects "mastery" of differentiation. • Focuses on the challenges instead of the benefits/necessity. • Seeks solutions that are already part of a repertoire of strategies instead of redefining the nature of curriculum and instruction. • Identifies the challenges inherent in high-prep differentiation (grading major projects) instead of focusing on low-prep possibilities. • Lacks a big-picture understanding of the philosophy due to misperceptions about good curriculum and instruction (e.g., assessment and evaluation). • Lacks persistence and a willingness to work at understanding and application.	• Tolerates the ambiguous nature of differentiation. • Understands the philosophy of differentiation but lacks confidence in application. • Acknowledges gaps in personal understanding and skills with differentiating curriculum and instruction. • Makes surface-level connections between differentiation and other models and strategies inherent in good curriculum and instruction. • Demonstrates a willingness to work through challenges with some persistence. • Distinguishes between good curriculum and instruction and that which is differentiated. • Asks thoughtful questions about both the philosophy and the application. • Can accurately explain differentiation as a concept.	• Accepts the ambiguous nature of differentiation. • Demonstrates accuracy and confidence in explaining differentiation of curriculum and instruction. • Makes connections among various methods within a discipline to facilitate differentiation. • Understands the connections among content, process, product, and learning environment when differentiation is achieved in the areas of readiness, interest, and learning profile (or any combination of these areas). • Exhibits a belief in differentiation but lacks confidence at times in addressing challenges. • Recognizes and avoids the "quick fixes" to differentiating curriculum and instruction.	• Skillfully differentiates curriculum and instruction through the development of curriculum. • Models differentiation with fluency and flexibility in staff development and teaching situations. • Problem-solves in situations where differentiation is both necessary and difficult. • Articulates the rationale, philosophy, and "how to" of differentiation to a wide variety of audiences (e.g., parents, teachers, students, administrators). • Uses various methods from a variety of disciplines to facilitate the differentiation of curriculum and instruction. • Exhibits an unyielding belief in the necessity of differentiation for all students. • Seeks new methods that will facilitate refinement in the differentiation of curriculum and instruction. • Understands there is much left to learn in the area of differentiation.

Source: Adapted from "Staff Differentiation Must Be Made to Measure," by K. A. Hedrick, 2005. *Journal of Staff Development, 26*(4), pp. 34–37. Reprinted with permission of the National Staff Development Council, www.nsdc.org, 2006. All rights reserved.

Part Two

Part Two

A Differentiation Rubric: Planning for Teacher Growth

What Does the Learner Need at Each Stage?

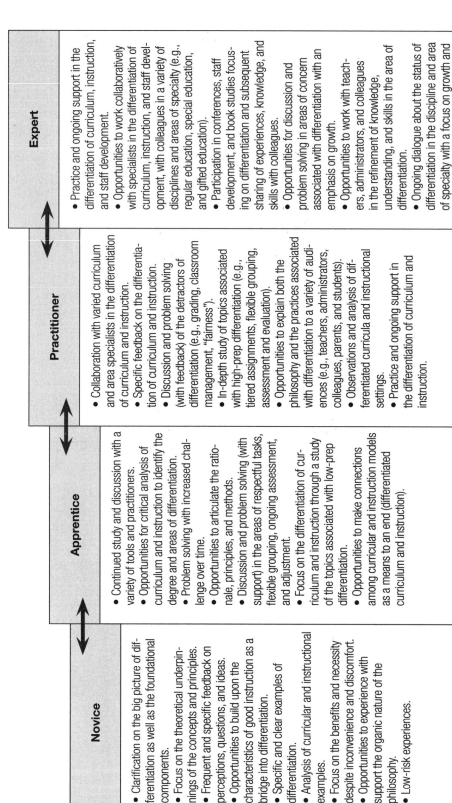

Novice	Apprentice	Practitioner	Expert
• Clarification on the big picture of differentiation as well as the foundational components. • Focus on the theoretical underpinnings of the concepts and principles. • Frequent and specific feedback on perceptions, questions, and ideas. • Opportunities to build upon the characteristics of good instruction as a bridge into differentiation. • Specific and clear examples of differentiation. • Analysis of curricular and instructional examples. • Focus on the benefits and necessity despite inconvenience and discomfort. • Opportunities to experience with support the organic nature of the philosophy. • Low-risk experiences.	• Continued study and discussion with a variety of tools and practitioners. • Opportunities for critical analysis of curriculum and instruction to identify the degree and areas of differentiation. • Problem solving with increased challenge over time. • Opportunities to articulate the rationale, principles, and methods. • Discussion and problem solving (with support) in the areas of respectful tasks, flexible grouping, ongoing assessment, and adjustment. • Focus on the differentiation of curriculum and instruction through a study of the topics associated with low-prep differentiation. • Opportunities to make connections among curricular and instruction models as a means to an end (differentiated curriculum and instruction).	• Collaboration with varied curriculum and area specialists in the differentiation of curriculum and instruction. • Specific feedback on the differentiation of curriculum and instruction. • Discussion and problem solving (with feedback) of the detractors of differentiation (e.g., grading, classroom management, "fairness"). • In-depth study of topics associated with high-prep differentiation (e.g., tiered assignments, flexible grouping, assessment and evaluation). • Opportunities to explain both the philosophy and the practices associated with differentiation to a variety of audiences (e.g., teachers, administrators, colleagues, parents, and students). • Observations and analysis of differentiated curricula and instructional settings. • Practice and ongoing support in the differentiation of curriculum and instruction.	• Practice and ongoing support in the differentiation of curriculum, instruction, and staff development. • Opportunities to work collaboratively with specialists in the differentiation of curriculum, instruction, and staff development, with colleagues in a variety of disciplines and areas of specialty (e.g., regular education, special education, and gifted education). • Participation in conferences, staff development, and book studies focusing on differentiation and subsequent sharing of experiences, knowledge, and skills with colleagues. • Opportunities for discussion and problem solving in areas of concern associated with differentiation with an emphasis on growth. • Opportunities to work with teachers, administrators, and colleagues in the refinement of knowledge, understanding, and skills in the area of differentiation. • Ongoing dialogue about the status of differentiation in the discipline and area of specialty with a focus on growth and development of expertise. • Support in the development and monitoring of policies and procedures that promote the differentiation of curriculum, instruction, and staff development.

Source: Adapted from "Staff Differentiation Must Be Made to Measure," by K. A. Hedrick, 2005, *Journal of Staff Development, 26*(4), pp. 34–37. Reprinted with permission of the National Staff Development Council, www.nsdc.org, 2006. All rights reserved.

A Differentiation Rubric: Planning for Teacher Growth

Activity

Directions:

- Refer to the Ascending Intellectual Demand: Differentiation rubric. Where are *you* in terms of expertise in differentiation? Where are the teachers you work with?
- Study the What Does the Learner Need at Each Stage? rubric to help you see a variety of ways to support teachers at different stages of expertise.
- Complete the chart below:
  - In the "Teacher's Name" column, write the names of several teachers you work with. If possible, choose teachers who are at different levels of comfort with differentiated instruction.
  - In the "Current Level of Expertise" column, write the level (novice, apprentice, practitioner, expert) that best matches what you have seen with this teacher. Use descriptors from Hedrick's rubric, or choose your own.
  - In the "Evidence" column, provide specific evidence for your determination if at all possible.
  - In the last column, write ideas for a specific plan of action that will support each teacher in moving closer to the expert level or in refining their skills as an expert.

Teacher's Name	Current Level/ Specific Descriptor	Evidence	Plan of Action/Next Steps for Growth

A Differentiated Lesson Observation Rubric

ACTION TOOL

Rationale and Purpose

When observing a teacher in a differentiated classroom, use this rubric to help identify his or her level of expertise with specific elements of a successful differentiated classroom. Then, use the rubric to help develop goals for professional development.

Directions

- Share the Differentiated Classroom in Balance mobile with administrators and staff development leaders.
- Distribute the rubric and the tool to administrators and staff development leaders. Discuss ways in which the rubric helps identify a range of teacher behaviors that support the elements of a differentiated classroom. Remind them that for differentiation to remain a district or school focus, teacher feedback should always include a discussion of differentiated practices.
- Encourage leaders to use the rubric as a tool for observation and for debriefing with teachers following an observation.

Tips and Differentiation Options

- Use the whole rubric or only selected rows when observing in a classroom.
- Share the mobile visual and the rubric with teachers before your visit so they know what you are looking for.

What to Look For

Thoughtful consideration of teacher level of expertise based on specific observations rather than just general impressions.

A Differentiated Lesson Observation Rubric

Mobile: A Differentiated Classroom in Balance

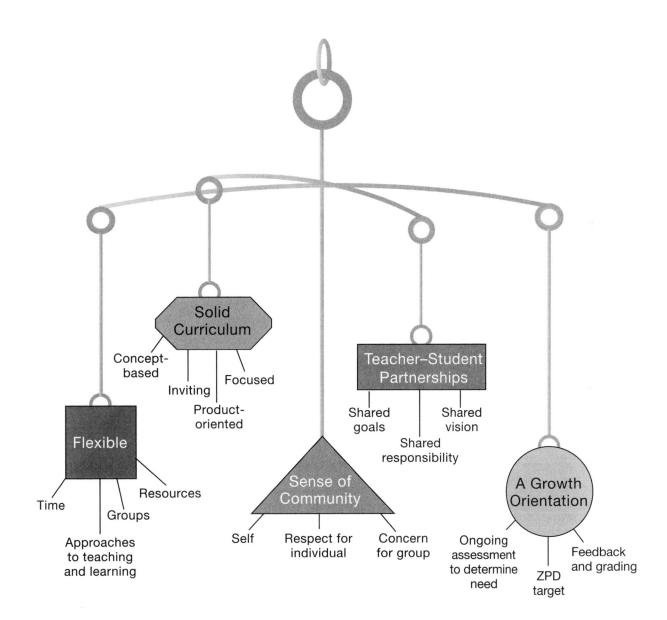

Source: Adapted with permission from the work of Carol Ann Tomlinson, Curry School of Education, University of Virginia.

A Differentiated Lesson Observation Rubric

Activity

Directions:

- Use the rubric or parts of the rubric below to help you determine the level of expertise in differentiation that a teacher displays during a classroom visit.
- Use the rubric to set professional development goals after a classroom visit, and complete the reflection that follows the rubric for each teacher you observe.

Characteristics	Novice Level	Apprentice Level	Practitioner Level	Master Level
(Based on Carol Ann Tomlinson's "A Differentiated Classroom in Balance" mobile)	This is what we hope not to see. If we do, we need to help these teachers understand what good teaching and learning are all about.	These teachers are beginning to make sense of differentiated teaching and learning. They just need more support and practice.	This is where most good teachers who use differentiation are most of the time. These teachers have a pretty good handle on differentiation but would benefit from problem-solving sessions with one another or an expert.	Very few teachers will fall consistently into this category. Those who do are ready to lead and support others. Don't forget that they still need opportunities to refine their own knowledge, understanding, and skill. No one is ever done learning.
Solid Curriculum	• The lesson is unfocused or disorganized. Lesson goals are not listed. It is not clear what the teacher wants students to know, understand, and be able to do as a result of the learning experience. • Lesson components are not engaging and do not connect to students' lives. Students do not use what they learn. No differentiation takes place.	• The lesson has an identifiable structure, although the logic of that structure may be unclear. Student goals or objectives are listed but not referenced during the lesson, *or* these goals do not appear to match lesson components. • Lesson components are somewhat interesting to learners but do not necessarily connect with their lives or goals. Students use what they learn, but not in ways that require consistent use of high-level thinking skills. Differentiation takes place in a limited manner. Not all versions of an activity lead to the same KUD.	• The lesson is organized sensibly. It is clear to observer and students what students are to know, understand, and be able to do as a result of the learning experience. • Lesson components are engaging to learners and connect with their lives and/or goals. Students use what they learn in interesting ways that call upon higher-order thinking skills throughout the lesson. Differentiated activities relate to the same KUD.	• The curriculum is organized in a coherent (organized, unified, and sensible) manner. It is crystal clear to both observers and students what the teacher wants students to know, understand, and be able to do as a result of the learning experience *and* how specific lesson components match these goals. • Lesson components are mentally and affectively engaging to learners and clearly connect with their lives or goals. Students use what they learn in important ways; deal with complex problems, ideas, issues, and skills; and think at high levels. Differentiated activities are clearly related to same lesson goals (KUD).

A Differentiated Lesson Observation Rubric

Activity (Cont.)

Characteristics	Novice Level	Apprentice Level	Practitioner Level	Master Level
Growth Orientation	• Activities appear to be designed with little regard to student readiness, interest, or learning profile. • Work is not demanding for the majority of students. Few students are likely to grow as a result of the learning activities	• Students with a particular level of readiness, interest, or learning profile will likely grow, but others will find it difficult or impossible to do so. • Work inconsistently challenges students or challenges only some students.	• Students with varied readiness, interest, or learning profiles have an opportunity to grow at some point during the lesson. • Work is consistently demanding, although a few students may be able to "wriggle out" of the highest quality of work.	• All students, no matter their level of readiness, interests, or learning profiles, are appropriately challenged. • Lesson is written in such a way that no students can "wriggle out" of the highest quality of work; rather they are propelled to do their best.
Flexible Grouping	• No variation in instructional strategies, modes of presentation; grouping strategies; or use of time, space, and materials.	• Evidence of variation exists in at least one of the following: instructional strategies; modes of presentation; grouping strategies; and use of time, space, or materials. However, flexibility appears to occur for the sake of variety more than from a desire to match specific student needs or serve lesson goals.	• Evidence of variation exists in one or more of the following: instructional strategies; modes of presentation; grouping strategies; and use of time, space, or materials. This flexibility appears to be in response to student need or lesson goals.	• A variety of instructional strategies, modes of presentation, and grouping strategies are evident. Time, space, and materials are used flexibly and creatively. Flexibility is in response to a clear analysis of student needs or perfectly serves learning goals.
Teacher–Student Partnerships	• The teacher's only role is to deliver content or direct student activities. • The teacher takes the lead in classroom activities. • The teacher sets goals and assesses student progress toward these goals.	• Teacher's role is primarily deliverer of information or director of student activities. • The teacher allows for occasional student input into lesson content and activities. • The teacher sets goals and assesses student progress toward these goals, but invites limited student input as to what the goals are or the progress they're making.	• Teacher plays the role of deliverer of information or director of student activity but also acts as coach or facilitator of learning at some point in the lesson. • Teacher frequently invites and encourages student input into lesson content and activities. • Students frequently work with teachers to set goals for learning and assess progress toward those goals.	• Teacher's overall role is primarily that of coach or facilitator of learning. • Students and teacher have consistent and balanced input into lesson content. • Students are consistently involved in setting goals for learning and assessing progress toward those goals, taking on increasing responsibility for their own learning.

A Differentiated Lesson Observation Rubric

Activity (Cont.)

Characteristics	Novice Level	Apprentice Level	Practitioner Level	Master Level
Sense of Community	• Environment is physically and emotionally unsafe. • There is no apparent focus on individual or group excellence and growth. • Students do not engage or support one another in learning. • Students recognize and comment negatively on differences. There are no discussions about the rationale for differentiation or related concerns.	• Environment is physically safe, but some students occasionally feel as though they do not belong or are not valued. • Focus tends to be on competition among students, rather than individual or group excellence and growth. • Students engage and support one another but tend to do so within their usual groups or cliques. • Occasional negative comments about differences are heard. Discussions about the rationale for differentiation or related concerns come up, but usually only when someone is unhappy.	• Environment is physically and emotionally safe. In general, students feel as they though they belong and are valued. • Individual and/or group excellence and growth appear to be valued. • Students generally engage and support one another in learning. They appear comfortable working with a variety of peers. • Students recognize and acknowledge similarities and differences in student needs. There are ongoing whole-class and individual discussions about the rationale for differentiation. Concerns about fairness and questions about different tasks are handled immediately and sensitively	• Environment is physically and emotionally safe. There are consistent affirmations by both teacher and students of belonging and value. • Students and teacher consistently focus on both individual and group excellence and growth. • Students consistently engage and support one another in learning. They are perfectly comfortable working with any other student in the class. • Students and teacher recognize, acknowledge, and celebrate similarities and differences. Ongoing whole-class and individual discussions about the rationale for differentiation take place. Concerns about fairness and questions about different tasks occasionally occur, but there is little need for them because differentiation is so keenly integrated into the class philosophy and belief system of both teacher and students.

A Differentiated Lesson Observation Rubric

Activity (Cont.)

Reflections About My Observation

1. In general, I think this teacher operates at the _____ level because _____

_____

_____

_____

2. I will help this teacher further his or her growth by:

    •

    •

    •

    •

Tools for Teachers

Tools for Teachers

Part Three

SECTION 1: EVALUATING READINESS, INTEREST, AND LEARNING PROFILE

Teacher Pre-assessment for Differentiation (Readiness)

ACTION TOOL

Rationale and Purpose

To make staff development responsive to teacher needs, the school leadership must determine individual teachers' specific background knowledge with respect to differentiation. In this way, leaders provide staff development that will honor teachers' current level of knowledge, understanding, and skill and help them move forward in their journeys toward expertise in differentiation. Use this tool to activate teacher background knowledge with respect to differentiation.

Directions

- Explain that this tool is used to activate participants' background knowledge.
- Distribute one copy of the pre-assessment to each teacher.
- Tell teachers they may fill out the chart using any combination of words, symbols, and pictures.
- Provide them with enough time to complete the graphic organizer (10–15 minutes).
- Collect the pre-assessment, and analyze the results. Use the results to inform future professional development sessions.

Tips and Differentiation Options

- The more background knowledge teachers have in differentiated instruction, the longer they will need to complete the pre-assessment.
- Remind teachers that it is OK if they do not have much to write. It is also OK to write things they are not sure about. Remind them that you are pre-assessing background knowledge to ensure that the staff development you will provide best meets the needs of teachers at all levels of familiarity with differentiation.
- For an extra layer of analysis, you might ask teachers to star or circle the answers of which they are absolutely sure.
- For specific planning for differentiated staff development, it is best to have teachers complete the chart individually. However, if you prefer, you may ask teachers to complete the activator on chart paper in small groups of 3–4 as part of a workshop opening or discussion on differentiation. This will foster important discussion that can inform you about their background and beliefs. Circulate as they work so that you can hear their comments. Jot down any comments you wish to address as a whole group or to use for planning purposes.

- Make a plan for addressing teachers' "burning questions" over time in your training sessions. When you do address these questions or provide differentiated staff development based on teacher responses to the activator, point it out to teachers. This helps them understand the purpose of the activator and the importance of follow-up based on pre-assessment.

What to Look For

Definition

- The best answers will center on assessing and then meeting students' varied interest, learning profile, and readiness needs in the classroom as often as possible in the context of a high-quality curriculum, a strong sense of community, and a focus on growth over time.
- Watch out for the common misconception that in a differentiated classroom, teachers are expected to meet **all** student needs **all** of the time.
- Note whether or not teachers use the term *readiness* or *ability*. This will indicate whether or not you need to clarify the difference between these terms. *Readiness* is a much broader term than *ability*. In addition to any innate ability a student may have, *readiness* also considers students' background knowledge, their physical and emotional development and current health, their attitude toward learning in general or toward the specific subject or topic, their past successes or challenges with the material or school in general, and so forth.

Associated Vocabulary

Advanced answers will include terms such as *readiness, interest, learning profile, content, process, product, learning styles, multiple intelligences, concepts, understandings, KUD, pre-assessment, formative assessment, summative assessment, flexible grouping, challenge, engagement, growth,* and *respectful activities.*

Examples

Advanced answers will center on describing a classroom that is flexible, focuses on key curriculum goals (such as standards), and provides a place for teachers and students to work together to provide engaging and challenging work for all.

Nonexamples

- Advanced answers refer to one-size-fits-all classrooms where the teacher functions primarily as the giver of information and the students as passive receptors and where teachers hold students to differing standards based on preconceived notions of their abilities.
- If teachers write "whole-group work," you will need to remind them that whole-group work is part of a differentiated classroom, too. A better answer would be "*only* whole-group instruction."

Part Three

Teacher Pre-assessment for Differentiation

Activity

Complete the chart to show what you know about differentiation. Write as much as you can.

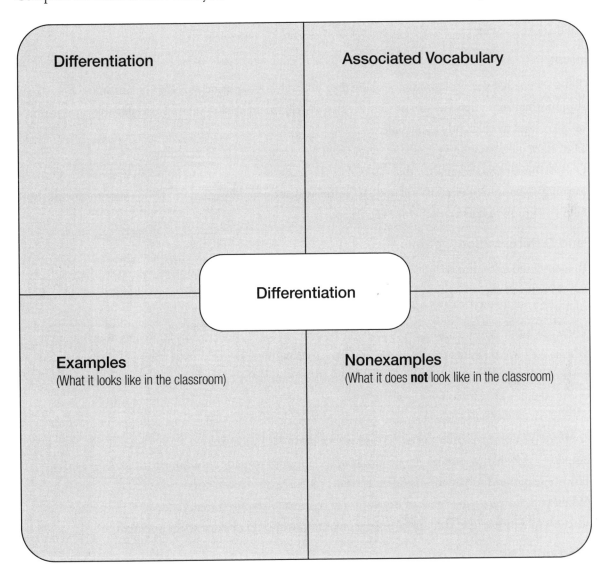

On the back of this sheet, please list specific "burning" questions you have about differentiated instruction.

Staff Development Learning Preferences Survey

Rationale and Purpose

This tool helps you gather information about teachers' learning preferences.

Directions

- Tell teachers that you wish to find out how they like to learn about new models in education. You need this information so that you can make your staff development sessions as useful as possible and help teachers learn as efficiently as possible.
- Distribute the survey, and provide time for them to complete it (10–15 minutes).
- Collect the surveys and analyze the results. Use the results of the survey to help you identify the kinds of learning options to offer your staff as they explore differentiated instruction. This information will also help you group teachers together for specific purposes.

Tips and Differentiation Options

- Remember to ask a question on the survey only if you are likely to offer options based on the result. For example, if you do not have a choice in the time of day to offer staff development, then don't ask question 4.
- There are lots of commercial surveys available by a variety of authors (Silver & Strong, Renzulli, Myers-Briggs, etc.). If you are going to use a particular survey with students in your school or district, you might wish to use a similar survey with teachers. For example, the Kaleidoscope Profile (www.plsweb.com/resources/kaleidoscope) is available in student and adult versions. If the survey you use is self-scorable, have teachers share their results with their grade-level or subject-area colleagues if they feel comfortable doing so. (Allow them to pass if they don't wish to share.)
- As part of this sharing or later as a whole group, point out any patterns among the faculty. Ask them how these patterns might affect student learning in their school or district.
- When you provide follow-up staff development options related to the survey results, point these out to teachers to reinforce the idea that pre-assessment results should directly affect instruction.

What to Look For

- Responses to Question 1 indicate:
    - a. preference for visual learning via text
    - b. preference for auditory learning
    - c. preference for visual learning
    - d. preference for kinesthetic learning

- Responses to Question 2 indicate (See Sternberg & Grigorenko, 2007.):
  - a. preference for analytical thinking
  - b. preference for practical thinking
  - c. preference for creative thinking
- Take note of the diversity of styles in particular teams or departments. The more diversity in a team or department, the easier it will be for members to work together to design activities that match a variety of learning preferences.

Part Three

Staff Development Learning Preferences Survey

Activity

Circle the answer that best completes each statement.

1. When learning about a new model or strategy in education, I prefer to
    a. Read about it.
    b. Hear about it.
    c. See it in action.
    d. Try it out on my own.

2. When learning about a new model or strategy in education, I first
    a. Focus on the details and structure of the model or strategy.
    b. Try to figure out how the model or strategy would look in my own classroom.
    c. Use the ideas as a springboard for my own variation on the model or strategy.

3. When learning about a new model or strategy in education, I prefer to
    a. Learn on my own.
    b. Learn with others.

4. I am at my best in learning in
    a. Early morning.
    b. Mid-morning.
    c. Mid-afternoon.
    d. Late afternoon.

How interested are you in the following? (1 = I would prefer not to participate; 2 = I might participate; 3 = I would be very likely to participate)

____ Sharing examples of differentiated activities from my own classroom at a faculty meeting

____ Sharing examples of differentiated activities from my own classroom at a department or team meeting

____ Allowing colleagues to observe me teaching a differentiated activity

____ Observing colleagues teaching a differentiated activity

____ Watching videos of differentiation in action, followed by a discussion of what is seen

____ Being part of a book study on differentiation

____ Attending a local conference on differentiation

____ Taking a course in differentiation

Part Three

What's My Role? (Learning Profile)

Rationale and Purpose

This activity will both gather information about teachers' learning preferences and serve to educate teachers about the impact learning preferences can have on students' success.

Directions

- Before beginning, gather the following materials:
  - Chart paper and markers
  - Drawing paper and colored pencils
  - Computers for word processing that are connected to a printer (optional)
  - Blank paper for those who prefer to write instead of using a computer
  - A selection of Lego blocks (or other model-building materials)
  - A box of "props" for the skit (hats, household items, etc.) (optional)
- Ask teachers to rank their skill in the following, with 1 as the skill they are best at:
  - Writing a story
  - Drawing a picture
  - Acting
  - Building with Lego blocks
- Designate a corner of the room for each skill, and ask teachers to move to the corner that corresponds to their *best* skill. Pause briefly to let them share in corner groups why they chose that skill as their best. Then, ask them to move to the corner that designates the skill they do *least* well. Again, pause for a brief sharing. Have them remain in these groups for Round 1. (Note the reaction of participants when you announce this. They will likely groan.)
- Distribute the direction sheet for Round 1. Tell teachers they will be working in small groups to accomplish a task. Divide the teachers in each corner into reasonably sized work groups (3–5 people), and allow 20–30 minutes for them to complete the assignment. Inform them of the time constraints.
- Ask groups to share their completed projects. As groups share, the audience members should individually assess the quality of the product. Tell them that they will not have to share their evaluation with others.
- Repeat the exercise by asking teachers to return to the corner of the room that represents their *best* skill. Distribute the direction sheet for Round 2. Provide the same amount of time as in Round 1.
- Once again, ask groups to present and individuals to evaluate the projects.
- Distribute the discussion sheet, and debrief the experience.

Tips and Differentiation Options

- Note that, by asking teachers to design products that communicate the most important ideas about the topic, you are reinforcing their understanding of Understand statements. [See the KUD Sort (p. 81) and Tiered KUD Application Activities (p. 85).]
- Depending on your audience, you may substitute other assignment topics if you prefer. Pick something teachers are likely to be familiar enough with to identify key ideas.
- You may substitute other skills for the groups (e.g., musician, storyboarder). Ensure that the tasks are different enough to tap into a variety of learning styles or multiple intelligences.
- Depending on the time available, you may break this activity up into two parts. Round 1 may be completed in one session, with Round 2 and discussion in a follow-up session.
- The final discussion may occur as a whole group or in small groups. If you use small groups, regroup participants so that discussion group members represent a mixture of learning preferences.

What to Look For

- During each round, circulate and take note of:
  - How quickly and efficiently groups get started.
  - Who (if anyone) emerges as a group leader.
  - The kinds and amount of participation among group members.
- Work will likely be more efficient and enthusiastic in Round 2. Expect complaints during Round 1.
- The products in Round 2 will likely be superior to those in Round 1.

Part Three

What's My Role?

Activity

Round 1

- Imagine that we have been studying the pilgrims. You and your teammates will now prepare a presentation to help us see what you have learned in this unit. Your project must clearly communicate the three most important ideas you think people should remember about the pilgrims. You may use the provided supplies and anything you have with you today. You will share your project when the time is up.
- While you watch the other groups present, evaluate their work using the criteria below. (You will not have to share your evaluations with others.)
- For each project, please indicate on a scale of 1–4 (with 4 being the best):
  - The importance of the ideas communicated.
  - How well the project communicated those ideas.
  - The technical quality of the project.

Round 2

Form new groups as directed by your leader, and repeat this exercise using pioneers as your new topic.

Discussion

Discuss the following questions, and record your thoughts:

1. How did you react when you were asked to move from the corner that corresponded to your best skill to the corner designated for your weaker skill? How does that experience relate to how students feel when they are assigned to work in their most and least preferred ways of learning?

2. Consider the similarities and differences between the two experiences with learning profile.

Part Three

What's My Role?

Activity (Cont.)

3. In looking at your grading of the projects, what differences in quality, if any, did you notice?

4. Compare your feelings about each of the two experiences.

5. What can we conclude from this experience about the importance of learning profile differentiation?

Differentiated Instruction Interest Survey

Rationale and Purpose

This tool will help you gather information about teacher interests related to differentiated instruction.

Directions

- Tell teachers that there will be times when they may choose which aspect of differentiated instruction practices to focus on. You wish to know their interests ahead of time so that you can provide appropriate staff development options and determine possible study groups.
- Allow 5–10 minutes for teachers to complete the survey.

Tips and Differentiation Options

- Tailor the survey to those options you are able to offer in upcoming staff development sessions. In general, you want to be able to use the information you collect as soon as possible after giving the survey, so don't offer options you are unlikely to provide. For example, if you do not intend to teach the RAFT strategy, do not include that in Question 2.
- The results of Question 3 would be useful in designing a jigsaw of readings about differentiation.
- Question 5 might provide you with other ideas for staff development topics, as well as information about specific coaching needs.

What to Look For

- Take note of the diversity of responses, and use the results to form study or discussion groups.
- Teachers tend to feel more comfortable with certain aspects of differentiation than others. It is perfectly fine for them to begin their differentiation "journeys" with a focus on interest or learning profile or readiness differentiation. Over time, of course, you will need to see that all teachers become comfortable with all aspects of differentiation.

Differentiated Instruction Interest Survey

Activity

Please indicate the answer that best completes the following statements.

1. I am most interested in learning more about
    a. Interest differentiation.
    b. Learning profile differentiation.
    c. Readiness differentiation.
    d. How to incorporate more than one kind of differentiation into an activity.

2. I am most interested in the following strategy for differentiation:
    a. RAFTs
    b. Sternberg intelligence preferences
    c. Learning centers
    d. Learning contracts
    e. Tiered lessons

3. I prefer to read
    a. An overview of the components of differentiated instruction.
    b. About the theory and rationale behind differentiation.
    c. Examples of how differentiation looks in the classroom.
    d. About the results of implementing differentiated instruction.

4. I am most interested in expanding my repertoire of
    a. Pre-assessment strategies.
    b. Ongoing assessment strategies.
    c. Summative assessment strategies.

5. The aspect of differentiation I am most interested in learning more about is _____ _____ because _____ _____ _____.

Tools for Teachers

SECTION 2: WRITING KNOW, UNDERSTAND, AND DO GOALS

Part Three

KUD Sort

ACTION TOOL

Rationale and Purpose

This tool will help teachers recognize the difference between the "Know," the "Understand," and the "Be Able to Do" goals of a lesson.

Directions

- Download the KUD Sort cards and answer keys from www.ascd.org/downloads, using the key code on p. vi.
- Prepare the KUD cards by placing each boxed statement, organized by subject area (Science, for example), on a separate index card. Print one copy of the answer key for each corresponding set of cards.
- Place the KUD cards (including the three Know, Understand, and Be Able to Do header cards) and the folded answer key into a baggie or some other container. This will constitute one "set." Repeat for other subject areas.
- Make a set of cards and answer keys for every 3–4 people in your workshop.
- Distribute one set to each group. Post or provide the instructions for the activity.
- Debrief: What was hard about this activity? Easy? How can we tell the difference between a Know goal and an Understand goal?

Tips and Differentiation Options

- Use a different color of card for each subject area.
- Consider whether you want teachers to work in their subject area or in a subject area that is less familiar. (Less familiar is generally a bit trickier.) You could also distribute the sets of cards at random.
- If you prefer, use your own state or provincial standards in place of the examples provided. Be sure you have a balance of Know, Understand, and Do goals. Some standards documents are light on the Understand goals. For these you may need to go to Web sites such as the National Council of Teachers of Mathematics (http://standards.nctm.org) to find suitable "big ideas."
- To support teachers new to KUD work, provide the following as a scaffold. The material in brackets is a bit of a giveaway, so you may not want to include that in your scaffold.
  - Know goals: Facts, dates, vocabulary, definitions, key places, key people. [Usually stated in a bulleted list.]
  - Understand goals: Overarching statements or "truths" about the discipline(s), principles, generalizations, theories, "big ideas." [Usually written as a complete sentence: "I want students to understand that . . ."]

- Do goals: Processes, skills of the discipline(s), what students should be able to do at the end of the learning experience. [Begin with an observable verb and closely relate to behavioral objectives.]
- Instead of using cards for each bullet, you may hand out a sheet of paper with all the bullets from a particular subject. Ask each teacher to indicate next to the bullet whether the statement is a Know (K), Understand (U), or Do (D). Then, they may check their answers with the key. However, the kinesthetic aspect to the original version of this activity both is enjoyable for teachers and serves as a good model for varying teaching strategies.

What to Look For

- Most teachers quickly notice that the Do goals always begin with an observable verb. The Do goals are closely related to behavioral objectives familiar to many teachers.
- Sometimes teachers will argue about whether something is a Know goal or an Understand goal. Use your judgment—consider whether they are interpreting the statement as an overarching idea (U) or as an individual piece of information to memorize (K). For more help with the difference between knowledge and understanding, see the It's Probably an Understanding If It . . . chart (p. 87) or Wiggins and McTighe (2005), Chapter 2.
- Note those teachers who are struggling to differentiate between Know, Understand, and Do goals and those who seem to have an immediate grasp of the difference. Also listen for evidence of teachers who appear familiar with "big ideas" or use vocabulary from Understanding by Design, for example. Use this information to form groups for the Tiered KUD Application Activities that follow (p. 85).

KUD Sort

Activity

Directions:
- Remove **only** the package of cards from your baggie, place the **header cards** (Know, Understand, Do) on the table, and shuffle the rest of the cards.
- Sort the cards under the appropriate header:
  - KNOW (Knowledge)
  - UNDERSTAND (Big Ideas)
  - DO (Skills)
- When you are satisfied with your groupings, check your results with the answer key (in the baggie).
- Discuss any cards you miscategorized, and answer the reflection questions below.
- Reshuffle the cards before returning them to their baggie.

Reflection Questions:

1. What do the Know goals have in common?

   The Understand goals?

   The Do goals?

Part Three

KUD Sort

Activity (Cont.)

2. How would you explain the difference between a Know goal and an Understand goal?

3. Were there any categories you frequently confused? If so, how might you better distinguish between them in the future?

Source: Adapted with permission from an activity by Kristi Doubet, James Madison University.

Tiered KUD Application Activities

ACTION TOOL

Rationale and Purpose

Use this tool following the KUD Sort tool (p. 81) to help teachers at various of levels of readiness refine their ability to write coherent KUD goals.

Directions

- Tell teachers that you want them to work on an activity that will push them just a little beyond their current level of comfort with writing KUD goals. Because they are at different levels of familiarity with KUD, you have differentiated this activity by readiness. Explain that you used what you have learned about their comfort level with this process to assign them to one of three tiers:
  - Tier 1 is for those teachers who are still struggling with identifying "big ideas" and who are confused about the difference between Know goals and Understand goals.
  - Tier 2 is for teachers who recognize the different aspects of KUD planning and need practice writing objectives in this format.
  - Tier 3 is for teachers who have a background in KUD planning, Understanding by Design, or other models that focus on the big ideas of a discipline. It asks teachers to deepen their understanding of the role of each of the three types of goals and refine their ability to write cohesive KUD goals.
- Remind them that if they feel they have been assigned to the wrong tier, they should discuss it with you.

Tips and Differentiation Options

- If you prefer, you may let teachers self-select their tier according to their own evaluation of their readiness. Adults generally appreciate the opportunity to choose; however, you do run the risk that teachers won't choose appropriately. Emphasize that they should choose the tier that will push them just a little beyond their comfort zone without frustrating them.
- Offer teachers the option of working alone or with someone who teaches a similar curriculum. (Note that Tier 1 teachers particularly benefit from small-group brainstorming.)
- When teachers in Tiers 2 and 3 write their KUD plans, they may focus on a single lesson or on a unit of study. If they are having difficulty, suggest they think in terms of a unit. It will often be easier to come up with Understand goals for a larger time frame.
- Suggested follow-up activities:
  - Collect the KUD plans, and provide individual feedback.
  - Ask each teacher to present his or her KUD statements to a small group. Audience members should check to be sure the Understand statements are complete sentences and do or could begin with the phrase "I want students to understand that . . ." The audience should also verify that the Do

statements represent outcomes for the lesson or unit and not the classroom activities to help them get there (for example, "Use slope-intercept form to draw line" versus "Complete a worksheet on slope-intercept form").

- Circulate as teachers work and choose a few solid examples of Understand goals or completed KUD plans. Ask teachers to share these with the group. Discuss what makes each a good example.
- Provide time for teachers to refine their work in light of the follow-up activities.

What to Look For

- It is not necessary for there to be a one-to-one correspondence between the Know, Understand, and Do components. In fact, it is likely that there will be only a few Understand goals and many Know and Do ones.

- Check to see that each Understand goal is stated as a full sentence that does or could begin with, "I want students to understand that . . ." It is not correct, for example, to write, "I want students to understand algebra."

- The Do goals must be observable. It is not correct, for example, to write, "I want students to be able to understand the causes of the Gulf War."

- The Do goals are final outcomes of the unit or lesson and not the classroom activities that students complete. It is not correct, for example, to write, "I want students to be able to complete the worksheet on irregular verbs with 80 percent accuracy."

Tiered KUD Application Activities

Tier 1 Activity

In this activity, you will focus on writing Understand statements.

1. Study the examples and nonexamples of Understand statements in the chart below.

It's probably an Understanding if it . . .	Example	Nonexample
Represents subtle ideas that are not obvious at first glance	Scientists' unique social and educational backgrounds and differences lead to their disagreement about the interpretation of evidence or the development of a theory.	Scientists study the world around them.
Involves multiple layers or multiple meanings	Changing the grouping or the order of addends or factors does not change a sum or product.	$2 + 3 = 3 + 2$
Is an idea that is especially powerful in understanding the discipline and across topics in the discipline	A person's perspective is shaped in part by his or her past experiences.	The Hundred Years' War lasted from 1337 to 1453.
Provides a purpose for the discipline, the reason for studying the discipline, and an explanation for why the discipline is valuable	Dance is a form of communication.	American ballet has been shaped by George Balanchine.
Raises additional questions or paths of thought within the discipline	Use of specific art materials and style are related.	Monet was an impressionist.
Can be understood on a continuum; something that kindergarteners through graduate students could study, albeit at different levels of sophistication	Parts of a system are interrelated.	A system has more than one part.
Can be stated as "I want students to understand **that** . . .," rather than "I want students to understand . . ."	I want students to understand that voice is the writer revealed.	I want students to understand writer's voice.
Is a pithy statement that reveals a truth about the study or practice of the discipline	Culture shapes people and people shape culture. (This is something that anthropologists spend their lives studying!)	There are lots of cultures in the world.

Source: Adapted from *Tools for High-Quality Differentiated Instruction: An ASCD Action Tool* (pp. 78–79), by Cindy A. Strickland, 2007, Alexandria, VA: ASCD. Copyright 2007 by ASCD.

Part Three

Tiered KUD Application Activities

Tier 1 Activity (Cont.)

2. Brainstorm: What are the really big ideas in *your* discipline? In other words, if at the end of the year, students forgot the facts or got rusty on the skills, what would you at least want them to walk away understanding?

3. Star those big ideas that are the most important to you or that pertain to a particular unit of study. Place each big idea into the Understand column below. For at least **one** of your Understand statements, list what students would need to know and do to show their understanding. If you need help, refer to the KUD Basics chart on the next page.

KNOW	UNDERSTAND	DO

Tiered KUD Application Activities

Tier 1 Activity (Cont.)

KUD Basics

	Definition	Examples
Know	Most often represented in bullet form; sometimes as a sentence • Facts • Dates • Definitions • Rules • People • Places • Vocabulary • Information • Concepts	• There are 50 states in the United States. • Thomas Jefferson • 1492 • The Continental Divide • The multiplication tables • The rules of soccer • The parts of an engine
Understand	Best stated as a sentence beginning with "I want students to understand that . . ." • "Big" ideas • Essential understandings • Important (arguable) generalizations • Principals • Theories • The "point" of the discipline or the topic	• Multiplication is another way to do addition. • People migrate to meet basic needs. • All cultures contain the same elements. • Entropy and enthalpy are competing forces in the natural world. • Voice reflects the author. • Use of illegal drugs has both anticipated and unanticipated effects on the human body. • Composers use certain tools to change the mood of a piece of music. • Parts of a system are interdependent. • How you solve a problem depends on your perspective.

Do	The skills of a discipline, including:
	• Basic skills
	• Communication
	• Thinking:
	  – Analytical
	  – Critical
	  – Creative
	• Planning
	• Working
	• Evaluating
		• Analyze text for meaning
		• Solve a problem to find perimeter
		• Write a well-supported argument
		• Evaluate work according to specific criteria
		• Contribute to the success of a group or team
		• Use graphics to represent data appropriately
		• Sort buttons in two piles
		• Describe the job skills necessary for a given profession

Part Three

Tiered KUD Application Activities

Tier 2 Activity

In this activity, you will write a KUD plan for a lesson or unit of study. (If you teach more than one subject, work in your favorite subject area.)

1. Study the sample KUD plans in the table below. What is the relationship between the Know, Understand, and Do goal for each plan?

Sample KUD Plans

ELEMENTARY ART	SECONDARY ART
KNOW	KNOW
• Primary colors	• Primary and secondary colors found on the color wheel
UNDERSTAND	UNDERSTAND
• If you combine two primary colors, you make a new color.	• The color wheel arranges colors in a logical sequence, helping artists make informed decisions about the colors they use in a painting or other work of art.
BE ABLE TO DO	BE ABLE TO DO
• Tell what will happen if you mix two specific primary colors	• Use the color wheel to make and justify decisions for color choice and placement in a work of art

Tiered KUD Application Activities

Tier 2 Activity (Cont.)

ELEMENTARY SOCIAL STUDIES	SECONDARY SOCIAL STUDIES
KNOW • Places and roles in a community • Community vocabulary, including *need, want, goods, services* UNDERSTAND • People have needs and wants that are met by different roles within a community. BE ABLE TO DO • Explain the different components of a community • Compare, contrast, and evaluate community roles	KNOW • The elements of culture UNDERSTAND • All cultures contain some of the same elements. BE ABLE TO DO • Identify elements of culture in various settings and times • Recognize similarities and differences in cultures
ELEMENTARY SCIENCE	SECONDARY SCIENCE
KNOW • Vocabulary such as *precipitation, rain, drizzle,* and *snow* • The four main types of clouds UNDERSTAND • Natural signs can be used to predict the weather. • Clouds can be indicators of different weather. BE ABLE TO DO • Predict weather using knowledge of clouds • Identify the different types of clouds	KNOW • Parts of a cell UNDERSTAND • A cell is a system of interrelated parts. If one part breaks down, the whole cell suffers. BE ABLE TO DO • Identify the parts of a cell and describe their function

Part Three

Tiered KUD Application Activities

Tier 2 Activity (Cont.)

ELEMENTARY LANGUAGE ARTS	SECONDARY LANGUAGE ARTS
KNOW • Capital and lowercase letters • Letter sounds UNDERSTAND • Specific sounds correspond to letters in the alphabet. • Words are composed of letters. • The alphabet gives us a way to communicate. BE ABLE TO DO • Identify capital and lowercase letters • Identify and apply beginning sounds of words	KNOW • Elements of characterization UNDERSTAND • Passages from a text can reveal a character's personality. BE ABLE TO DO • Analyze character actions and statements
ELEMENTARY MATH	SECONDARY MATH
KNOW • Coin names and values UNDERSTAND • We can combine coins in different ways to make the same amount of money. BE ABLE TO DO • Given a supply of pennies, nickels, dimes, and quarters, combine the coins in more than one way to make a set amount of money (e.g., 40 cents)	KNOW • Geometry vocabulary UNDERSTAND • Using geometric terms is one way to describe the structure of our environment. BE ABLE TO DO • Describe, draw, compare, and classify geometric objects

Tiered KUD Application Activities

Tier 2 Activity (Cont.)

BUSINESS	**FOODS**
KNOW • Different forms of business ownership; definitions of key business terms UNDERSTAND • Each type of ownership presents unique advantages and disadvantages. BE ABLE TO DO • Select and explore a form of business ownership that complements their personal characteristics; explain the inner workings of one business form	KNOW • Macronutrients, calorie intake, ratio of body mass to fat • Foods that are healthy for teens UNDERSTAND • Keeping your body healthy involves an understanding of the roles of nutrition and exercise. BE ABLE TO DO • Evaluate personal diet and exercise regimen to maximize health
PHYSICAL EDUCATION	**MUSIC**

KNOW
 	
• How to dribble and pass
 	
UNDERSTAND
 	
• Practice makes better!
• There is more than one way to get better at a skill.
 	
BE ABLE TO DO
 	
• Improve skill in dribbling and passing
	KNOW
	
	• Circle of fifths
	
	UNDERSTAND
	
	• The circle of fifths provides a shortcut for figuring how to identify key signatures, find related keys, and determine the order of sharps and flats in a key signature.
	
	BE ABLE TO DO
	
	• Use the circle of fifths to
	   a. identify key signatures,
	   b. find related keys, and
	   c. add or subtract sharps and flats

Tiered KUD Application Activities

Tier 2 Activity (Cont.)

FRENCH GRAMMAR	FRENCH LITERATURE
KNOW	**KNOW**
• Definition of *verb* and *subject*	• Author of *Le Petit Prince* and overview of his life experience
• How to conjugate verbs	• Characters, setting, plot, and themes of *Le Petit Prince*
UNDERSTAND	• New vocabulary words
• Language is made up of patterns; if you can recognize the pattern, you can make a good guess about the form.	• Verb tenses used in text
BE ABLE TO DO	**UNDERSTAND**
• Conjugate verbs to match subjects	• Reading literature in the target language is one way to improve vocabulary and increase fluency.
	• It is possible to read for pleasure in more than one language!
	• As in native-language literature, we can see reflections of ourselves in target-language literature
	BE ABLE TO DO
	• Read fluently in target language
	• Demonstrate improved grammatical accuracy in writing and speaking
	• Incorporate new vocabulary into discussion and writings
	• Discuss literary elements in the target language
	• Analyze a theme found in the book
	• Examine your own beliefs and values through a textual lens

Tiered KUD Application Activities

Tier 2 Activity (Cont.)

2. Complete the KUD template for an upcoming unit or lesson.

KUD Template

Write what you want students to know, understand, and be able to do by the end of the learning experience. You may think in terms of a lesson or a unit of study.

KNOW (facts, dates, definitions, people, places, etc.)

-
-
-
-
-
-

UNDERSTAND (I want students to understand that . . .)

-
-
-

BE ABLE TO DO (specific skills; start with a verb; **not** classroom activities)

-
-
-
-

Part Three

Tiered KUD Application Activities

Tier 3 Activity

The best KUD plans are cohesive in nature. Although there tend to be fewer Understand statements than Know or Do ones, each Know or Do goal should be given a purpose and a context by at least one Understand statement. In this activity you will work to refine your ability to write coherent and cohesive KUD goals.

1. Study at least one of the sample unit KUD plans below. Check to be sure that every Know and Do statement has a corresponding Understand statement. If not, eliminate the Know or Do or add an appropriate Understand.

Sample Unit KUD Plan: English

KNOW (facts, dates, definitions, rules, people, places, etc.)

- General:
    - General literary vocabulary: *plot, setting, characters, theme, tone, point of view, protagonist, conflict*
    - Difference between text-to-text, text-to-self and text-to-world connections
- Specific to novel:
    - Author of *The Giver*
    - Characteristics of author's voice
    - Context of novel
    - Novel's plot, setting, characters, theme, tone, point of view, protagonist, conflict, climax

UNDERSTAND (big ideas, principles, generalizations, rules, the "point" of the discipline or topic within the discipline)

I want students to understand that . . .

- General:
    - Authors use specific tools when writing a novel.
    - All good novels include many of the same or very similar literary elements.
    - An author's voice is influenced by his or her own experiences and by the intended audience.
    - Literature is a reflection of ourselves and our society.
- Specific to novel:
    - Memory plays a key role in the continuation of a culture.
    - There is a relationship between pain and pleasure. If one is missing, the other is likely to also be missing.
    - Individuals can make a difference in a society.

Tiered KUD Application Activities

Tier 3 Activity (Cont.)

BE ABLE TO DO (skills of literacy, numeracy, communication, thinking, planning, production, etc.; start with a verb such as describe, explain, show, compare, synthesize, analyze, apply, construct, or solve)

- General:
  - Define the following literary elements: plot, setting, characters, theme, tone, point of view, protagonist, conflict
  - Explain what makes a "good" novel
  - Make text-to-text, text-to-self, and text-to-world connections
- Specific to novel:
  - Identify the novel's author and her context for writing the novel
  - Summarize the novel's plot
  - Identify the novel's setting, characters, theme, tone, point of view, protagonist, conflict
  - Evaluate the overall message of the novel

Sample Unit KUD Plan: Math

KNOW (facts, dates, definitions, rules, people, places, etc.)

- What data is and why we collect, interpret, and display it
- Different ways to display data: graphs and charts

UNDERSTAND (big ideas, principles, generalizations, rules, the "point" of the discipline or topic within the discipline)

I want students to understand that . . .

- You can pack a lot of information into a small space by using graphs and charts.
- There is usually more than one way to represent the same data.
- Some representations are more useful than others depending on the type of data, the intended audience, and the message to be communicated.

BE ABLE TO DO (skills of literacy, numeracy, communication, thinking, planning, production, etc.; start with a verb such as describe, explain, show, compare, synthesize, analyze, apply, construct, or solve)

- Collect data
- Analyze data
- Display data appropriately
- Interpret charts and graphs

Tiered KUD Application Activities

Tier 3 Activity (Cont.)

Sample Unit KUD Plan: Technology—Searching the Web

KNOW (facts, dates, definitions, rules, people, places, etc.)

- Common search engines and how they work
- How to make sense of the results
- What to look for when choosing sources

UNDERSTAND (big ideas, principles, generalizations, rules, the "point" of the discipline or topic within the discipline)

I want students to understand that . . .

- Different search engines produce different results due to the way they classify, sort, and prioritize information.
- The more you can refine your search parameters, the more useful the results.
- Not every Web site is created equal. The burden is on you, as the reader, to establish the validity, authorship, timeliness, and integrity of what you find.

BE ABLE TO DO (skills of literacy, numeracy, communication, thinking, planning, production, etc.; start with a verb such as describe, explain, show, compare, synthesize, analyze, apply, construct, or solve)

- Use common search engines
- Choose the appropriate search engine for a particular task
- Refine a general search to seek more specific information
- Evaluate the usefulness of a Web site as a resource

---

2. Complete the KUD Template on the next page for your own unit or lesson of study. Ensure that every Know or Do goal has a corresponding Understand goal to give it context and meaning.

Tiered KUD Application Activities

Tier 3 Activity (Cont.)

KUD Template

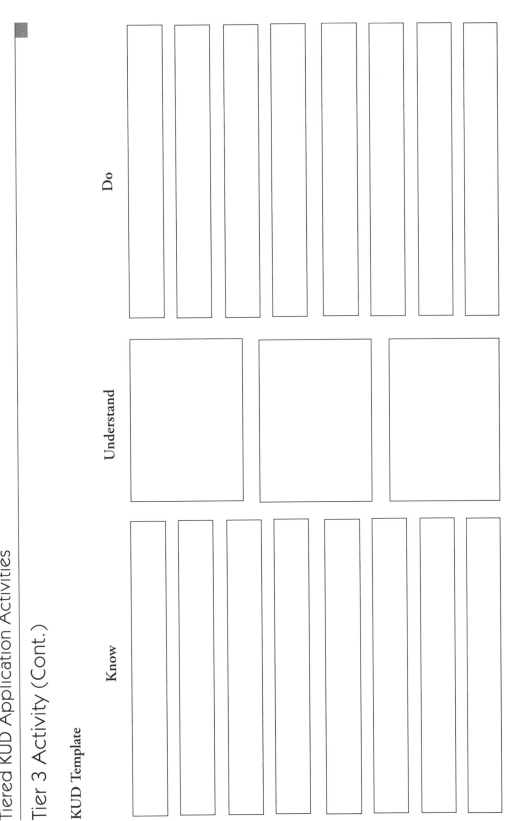

Know

Understand

Do

Source: Adapted with permission from *Tools for High-Quality Differentiated Instruction: An ASCD Action Tool* (p. 88), by Cindy A. Strickland, 2007, Alexandria, VA: ASCD. Copyright 2007 by ASCD.

Part Three

Tools for Teachers

SECTION 3: SUPPORTING TEACHER GROWTH IN ONGOING ASSESSMENT

Examining a Pre-assessment

Rationale and Purpose

This tool will help teachers identify the purpose and analyze the utility of sample pre-assessments.

Directions

- Remind teachers of how the results of their own pre-assessment for readiness, interest, and learning profile in differentiation have influenced staff development sessions so far and how they might influence future meetings.
- Explain that teachers do not have time to pre-assess everything in a unit of study. Therefore, they must learn to decide judiciously about what will be most helpful to include in a specific pre-assessment.
- Distribute the instructions to the activity and a copy of one of the provided sample pre-assessments to each teacher, or ask teachers to choose the pre-assessment that most interests them.
- Tell teachers to use the questions on the tool to help them analyze the pre-assessment on their own.
- Regroup teachers so they are working with others who studied the same pre-assessment. Ask them to share their analyses with one another.
- Finally, work as a whole group to form conclusions or big ideas about pre-assessment and its role in the differentiated classroom. Emphasize that the pre-assessment results should directly influence the instruction that follows.

Tips and Differentiation Options

- For a more in-depth study, have all teachers study the same pre-assessment. Use the questions in the tool as a catalyst for analysis. Repeat as needed.
- If you have copies of pre-assessments that your staff have used in their own classrooms, consider including them as samples. Ask the permission of the teachers involved.
- For additional sample pre-assessments, see *Tools for High-Quality Differentiated Instruction*: An ASCD Action Tool, pp. 159–165.

What to Look For

Sample analyses and suggested follow-up questions:

Sample 1

- Part 1 primarily tests the Know goals of the unit. Ask teachers for other ways they can think of to find out if students know the vocabulary, definitions, dates, people, and so forth for a similar unit.
- Part 2 questions definitely probe for understanding (as well as specific knowledge). Note how the teacher tries to connect the unit topics with student experience right from the start. Ask teachers to choose one of these questions and write three possible student responses: one that shows little or no

understanding, one that shows grade-level understanding, and one that shows advanced understanding. Offer the option of working alone or with a partner.

- In Part 3, both charts check for knowledge as well as probing understanding. In Chart A, point out that some students may know who but not why, or vice versa. Ask teachers how they would differentiate for the various combinations.

- Overall, this assessment appears to be pretty light on Do goals. Ask teachers "What Do goals, if any, does this assessment test for?" How could we pre-assess key Do skills for this unit? Also this assessment focuses mainly on readiness, although it will also give you cues about student connection to or interest in the topics. Ask teachers to suggest other test items they might add to this pre-assessment to further probe student readiness or assess related student interests and learning profiles.

Sample 2

- Questions 1 and 2 measure knowledge and skill in identifying parts. Another possibility that would focus more clearly on Do skills might be to ask students to draw a model of an atom and label its parts. Ask teachers for other ways they can think of to find out if students know the vocabulary, definitions, dates, people, and so forth for a similar unit.

- Questions 3–5 focus on understanding. Ask teachers to choose one of these questions and write three possible student responses: one that shows little or no understanding, one that shows grade-level understanding, and one that shows advanced understanding. Offer the option of working alone or with a partner.

- Questions 5 and 6 check on student interest, perhaps so the teacher can choose real-world applications of interest to students.

- Question 7 relates to student learning profile by assessing students' preferences for analytical, creative, or practical thinking. (For more information, see Sternberg & Grigorenko, 2007.) Ask participants how this question might be changed to measure students' preferences for visual, auditory, or kinesthetic learning; multiple intelligence preferences; or some other aspect of learning profile.

Sample 3

- Question 1 measures prior knowledge Ask teachers for other ways they can think of to find out if students know the vocabulary, definitions, dates, people, and so forth for a similar unit.

- Question 2 provides information on student knowledge of the typical grouping of instruments, provides insight into student skills in classification, and may provide insight into the understanding that there are similarities and differences in classes of instruments.

- Questions 3 and 4 reveal understanding. Some students will have a very simplistic answer, and others will have a more nuanced explanation. Ask teachers to choose one of these questions and write three possible student responses: one that shows little or no understanding, one that shows grade-level understanding, and one that shows advanced understanding. Offer the option of working alone or with a partner.

- Questions 5–7 measure student interest and background knowledge.

- Question 8 provides information about student learning preferences. For example, the teacher may offer students the option of exploring the concept of vibration by focusing either on the production or on the reception of sound. Ask participants how this question might be changed to measure students' preferences for visual, auditory, or kinesthetic learning; multiple intelligence preferences; or some other aspect of learning profile.

Examining a Pre-assessment

Sample 1: U.S. Government

Part 1: Identifications

Please identify the following. You do not have to write complete sentences. Indicate how sure you are of your answer with the following code: C= Confident; P= Pretty sure; G = Guess. If you have never heard of the term, write HLY (Haven't Learned Yet).

1. Balance of power:

2. Bill of Rights:

3. Civil rights:

4. Constitution:

5. Declaration of Independence:

6. Democracy:

7. Government:

8. Ideals:

9. Separation of powers:

Part 2: Short Answer

Answer the following with as much detail as you can.

1. Why should we learn about the Declaration of Independence, the Constitution, and the Bill of Rights?

2. What do these documents have to do with *your* life?

Examining a Pre-assessment

Sample 1: U.S. Government (Cont.)

3. What is a government? Why do we have one?

4. How is the U.S. government structured? Give as much detail as possible. You may write or diagram your answer.

5. What is the role of the U.S. Supreme Court? What is its importance to U.S. citizens?

Part 3: Charts

Fill in the charts below with as much information as you can.

Chart A:

	Declaration of Independence	Constitution	Bill of Rights
WHO wrote this document			
WHY this document was written			

Part Three

Examining a Pre-assessment

Sample 1: U.S. Government (Cont.)

Chart B:

Meaning— What does it mean to have rights? Inalienable rights?	Importance— Why do Americans care so much about rights?

CONSTITUTIONAL RIGHTS

Examples— Rights granted to us by the U.S. Constitution	Nonexamples— Rights not granted to us by the U.S. Constitution

What happens in the United States when a person's rights are violated? What *should* happen?

Why do you say so?

Source: From *The Parallel Curriculum in the Classroom, Book 2: Units for Application Across the Content Areas K–12* (pp. 271–272), by C. A. Tomlinson, S. N. Kaplan, J. H. Purcell, J. H. Leppein, D. E. Burns, & C. A. Strickland, 2005, Thousand Oaks, CA: Corwin. Copyright 2005 by Corwin Press. Reprinted with permission.

Examining a Pre-assessment

Sample 2: Science

1. In this diagram, identify the following:

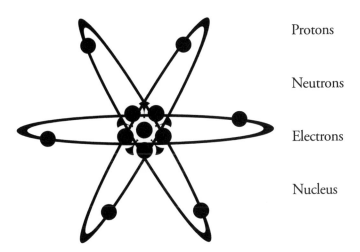

Protons

Neutrons

Electrons

Nucleus

2. What is this a diagram of?

3. What does it mean when we say the atom is a building block?

4. Why do scientists study atoms?

Part Three

Examining a Pre-assessment

Sample 2: Science (Cont.)

5. In what professions would it be important to know about atoms? Explain your thinking.

6. Circle the area of science that you are most interested in.

Biology   Chemistry   Physics

7. If you were asked to show how atoms join together to make molecules, which of the following would you choose? Why?
   - Diagram how and why atoms join to make molecules.
   - Write or tell a story about the making of a molecule.
   - Explain in pictures and/or words why understanding how atoms join together into molecules is important in the real world.

Examining a Pre-assessment

Sample 3: Music

1. Match each picture to its name.

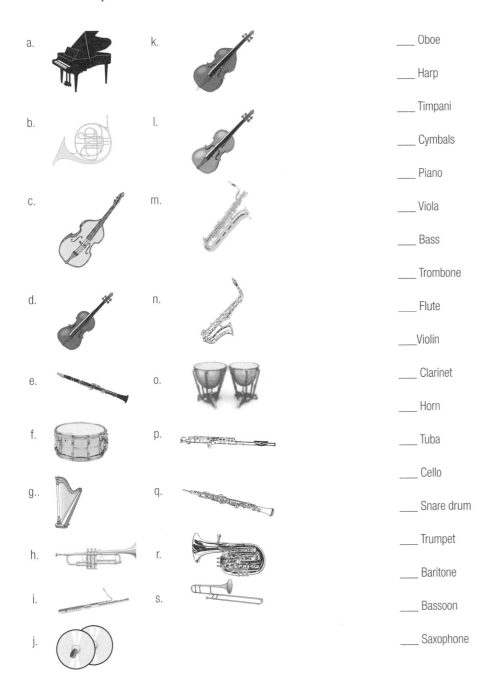

a.

k.

b.

l.

c.

m.

d.

n.

e.

o.

f.

p.

g..

q.

h.

r.

i.

s.

j.

___ Oboe

___ Harp

___ Timpani

___ Cymbals

___ Piano

___ Viola

___ Bass

___ Trombone

___ Flute

___ Violin

___ Clarinet

___ Horn

___ Tuba

___ Cello

___ Snare drum

___ Trumpet

___ Baritone

___ Bassoon

___ Saxophone

Part Three

Examining a Pre-assessment

Sample 3: Music (Cont.)

2. Organize the instruments into categories of your choosing. Explain why you organized them the way you did.

3. How do instrument(s) produce sound?

4. Why do orchestras or bands include so many different instruments?

5. What instrument(s) do you play? What instruments do members of your family play?

6. What instrument do you **wish** you could play? Why?

7. What kind of music do you listen to at home?

8. Would you rather play or sing a song or listen to a song?

Examining a Pre-assessment

Activity

Directions:

- Working alone, study one of the sample pre-assessments or a pre-assessment you or your colleagues have used in the past.
- Answer the following questions about your pre-assessment.

Pre-assessment I examined: _____

1. In what ways does the pre-assessment provide information about students' prior knowledge, understanding, and skill? About their interests? About how they like to learn?

2. What might you add to the pre-assessment if you were to adapt it for a similar unit? Why?

Examining a Pre-assessment

Activity (Cont.)

3. What might you eliminate if adapting it? Why?

4. Based on the results of the pre-assessment, what changes might you expect the teacher to make in the teaching of this unit?

5. Meet with others who studied the same pre-assessment. Share your analyses with one another. What insights did your peers have?

Part Three

Designing a Pre-assessment

ACTION TOOL

Rationale and Purpose

This tool will provide teachers the opportunity to design a pre-assessment for use in their own classrooms.

Directions

- Ask teachers to return to a unit KUD plan they have already written or write a new one.
- Ask teachers to identify key past or potential differences among students with respect to those objectives.
- Next, ask teachers to design an appropriate pre-assessment to check for these differences. They may use the flowchart and the Step-by-Step Planner provided in the tool to help them plan. (Novice differentiators would likely benefit most from the step-by-step version.)
- After teachers have completed their work ask:
    - What was most difficult about designing a pre-assessment?
    - What results do you anticipate?
    - What will you do if you get varied results?

Tips and Differentiation Options

- Allow teachers to work alone or with one or two others who teach the same unit.
- Don't let teachers begin to write a pre-assessment without first identifying the KUD goals for their unit.
- There is always too much to include on a pre-assessment for the time we have. Therefore it is important that teachers identify those Know, Understand, and Do goals that are most likely to reveal differences in student needs and are most crucial to success with the unit. It is also important to consider those areas of the curriculum that the teacher is most likely to be able to differentiate at this time (in terms of time and resources).
- Suggest that teachers administer their pre-assessment several days before the start of the unit so they have time to analyze and process the information.
- Remind teachers that they can break a pre-assessment into parts. They don't have to give it all at once.
- The best differentiated units usually incorporate readiness, interest, and learning profile differentiation. Therefore, encourage teachers to consider those aspects of student interest and learning profile that might affect student success in the specific unit and to include items that would measure these things.
- If teachers need help identifying the multiple ways students vary, distribute the Student Variance Reminder Card tool (available online only from www.ascd.org/downloads).
- Remind teachers that pre-assessments are rarely graded. This means they don't need to make extensive comments on the pre-assessments or even return them to students. Sometimes simply sorting

the pre-assessment into three knowledge, understanding, or skill piles—little or none, some, and advanced—will help teachers plan appropriate differentiation.

- The Sample Pre-assessment Recording Format is just one suggestion. The music teacher could also record information by filling out an index card for each student or simply sorting the pre-assessments into piles that represent the differences in student responses. For example, if she is going to teach about the instruments of the orchestra, she would only look at student responses to that section of the pre-assessment and sort the papers into three piles—above grade knowledge, on grade knowledge, and below grade knowledge. This gives her the appropriate groupings for that day's lesson.

- Ask teachers to administer their pre-assessments and bring sample results to the next meeting for analysis and discussion.

What to Look For

- The pre-assessment should reflect the unit KUD goals, though all of the KUD goals do not necessarily need to be tested.

- Be sure the pre-assessment is an appropriate length for the age of the students and the amount of time the teacher plans to designate for the assessment. We don't have time to pre-assess every aspect of a unit.

- Ensure that the pre-assessment measures knowledge, understandings, and skills that are truly central to success with the unit rather than ancillary information.

- In general, it is much easier to write test items that measure knowledge and skill. Ensure that teachers include at least one question that leads to information about student understanding.

- Experienced teachers often feel they know how a pre-assessment will turn out before they give it. Encourage them to pre-assess anyway; they may be surprised at individual results.

- Ensure that teachers recognize that a pre-assessment does no good if the results are varied, but the subsequent teaching is one-size-fits-all. Check to see that they have considered possibilities for appropriate follow-up differentiation.

Designing a Pre-assessment

Activity

Use the flowchart and Step-by-Step Planner below to help you to design a pre-assessment for an upcoming unit of study.

Flowchart

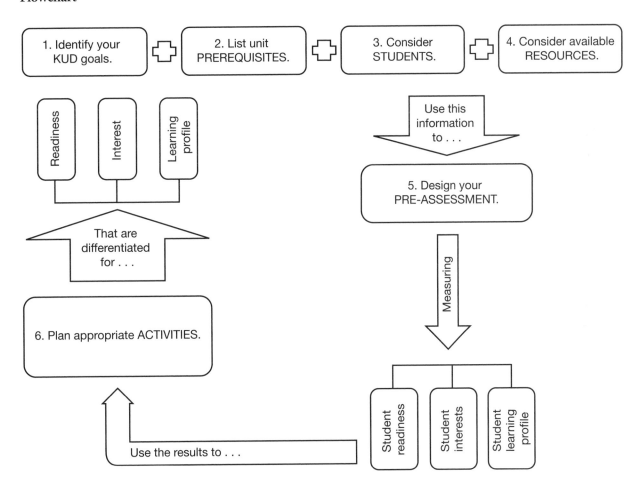

Part Three

Designing a Pre-assessment

Activity (Cont.)

Step-by-Step Planner

Step 1: Consider.

1. What is your unit KUD plan?

2. Which aspects of the KUD plan are the most important?

3. What prerequisite skills are necessary to be successful with this KUD plan?

4. Who are your students? How do they vary?

5. Of all the ways they vary, which differences are greatest?

6. For which student differences do you have or could you gather appropriate resources?

Designing a Pre-assessment

Activity (Cont.)

Step 2: Plan.

7. Sketch out possible pre-assessment items that would help you identify those differences in students **for which you are likely to differentiate.**

8. Ask a colleague to identify your purpose in including each item. Refine items as necessary.

9. Decide whether you will administer the pre-assessment as a whole or in pieces.

10. Plan a date or dates to administer the pre-assessment sufficiently in advance of the start of the unit so that you have time to interpret the results prior to planning instruction.

11. Administer the pre-assessment.

12. Evaluate and record the results in such a way that you can identify student differences for separate aspects of the KUD plan rather than recording an overall impression of student knowledge, understanding, and skill. For example, in recording results from the music pre-assessment, you might use the following format:

Designing a Pre-assessment

Activity (Cont.)

Sample Pre-assessment Recording Format

Instruments of the orchestra	AG = Above grade knowledge
	OG = On grade knowledge
	BG = Below grade knowledge
How instruments are grouped	1 = Knows traditional groupings and accurately places instruments into each category
	2 = Knows traditional groupings but makes minor mistakes in assigning instruments into categories
	3 = Does not know traditional groupings but groups instruments logically
	4 = Does not know traditional groupings and groups instruments illogically
How sound is produced	1 = Advanced understanding
	2 = Rudimentary understanding
	3 = Little or no understanding
Purpose of different instruments	1 = Advanced understanding
	2 = Rudimentary understanding
	3 = Little or no understanding
Background knowledge	1 = Plays an instrument
	2 = Family member plays an instrument
	3 = Does not play an instrument
Type of music preferred	Cl = classical
	Co = country
	P = pop
	Rk = rock
	Rp = rap
	Rg = religious
Performance preference	P = play
	S = sing
	L = listen

Designing a Pre-assessment

Activity (Cont.)

Sample Pre-assessment Summary

Student	Instruments of the orchestra	Instrument groupings	How sound is produced	Purpose of instruments	Background knowledge	Type of music preferred	Performance preference
Amanda	AG	2	1	2	2	P	L
Katie	AG	3	1	1	1	Rg	PSL
Matthew	OG	2	2	2	1	Rk	PL
Jessa	BG	3	3	3	3	Rk	SL

13. Use the pre-assessment results and other information to group students for appropriate differentiation. Remember that grouping does not necessarily mean students will work in a group. It may refer to how you mentally group students for the various versions of an activity. Use the following charts to help you plan.

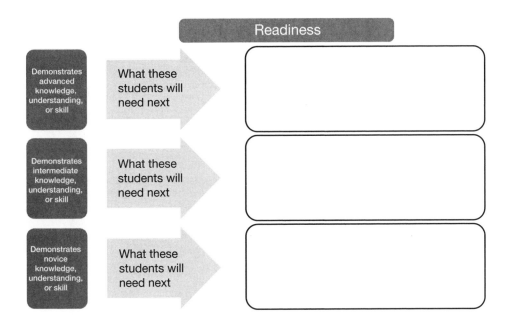

Readiness

Demonstrates advanced knowledge, understanding, or skill → What these students will need next →

Demonstrates intermediate knowledge, understanding, or skill → What these students will need next →

Demonstrates novice knowledge, understanding, or skill → What these students will need next →

Designing a Pre-assessment

Activity (Cont.)

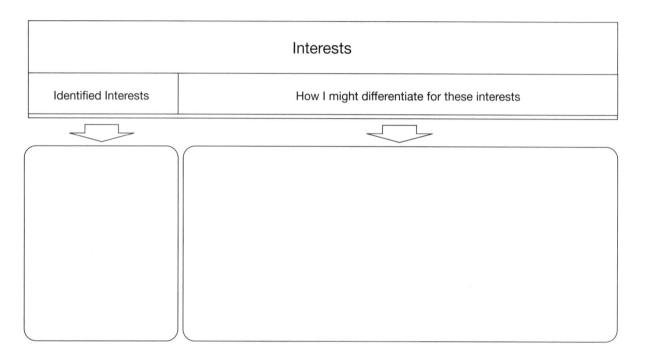

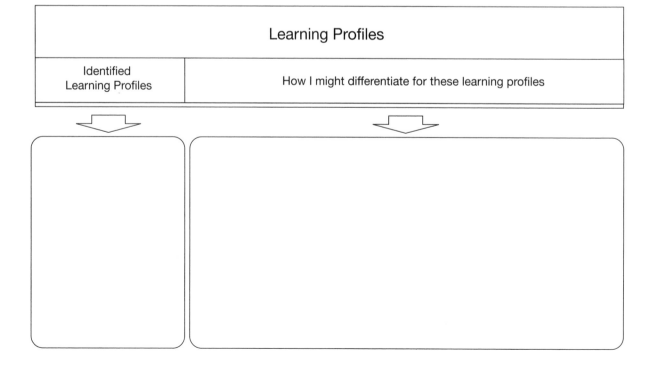

Using Formative Assessment Data to Plan for Differentiation

ACTION TOOL

Rationale and Purpose

This tool helps teachers practice using exit cards or journal prompts as a strategy for ongoing assessment and follow-up differentiation.

Directions

- Distribute the tool. Assign teachers specific rows, or ask them to choose two or three of the rows to work on. They should complete columns 2–4 for each of their rows.
- Ask teachers to share their work at their tables or in the large group.

Tips and Differentiation Options

- Instead of giving everyone the entire chart, make a copy of the tool, cut rows apart, and distribute one or two rows to each teacher. Allow teachers to work alone or with one or two others to complete the task.
- Assign rows based on the grade level of the teachers you are working with, their subject area(s) of interest, or the amount of time you have to devote to the process.
- Point out that this activity includes anchor activity possibilities (worthwhile activities that extend knowledge, understanding, or skill and can be completed independently while waiting for others to finish).
- If some teachers complete an anchor activity, ask them to share how they decided which anchor activity to complete, what they produced, and how they felt about completing an "extra" activity. Talk about the importance of making anchor activities interesting and useful to students.
- With the whole group, discuss the utility of anchor activities as a management technique for the differentiated classroom.

What to Look For

- If teachers are still having trouble identifying whether the prompt is designed to measure knowledge, understanding, or skill, revisit this concept with them, or distribute the KUD References tool (available online only from www.ascd.org/downloads) before they begin.
- One way to judge what is being measured is by the range of possible responses to the prompt. If there are only two possible responses—correct and incorrect— the prompt likely measures knowledge or skill. If there is a range of possible responses—novice, intermediate, advanced, expert—then it likely measures understanding.

Part Three

- Pay attention to the suggestions teachers make for follow-up differentiation. Be sure that the differentiated options lead to the same objective(s), are equally respectful, and help the students for whom they are assigned to grow as much and as quickly as possible.
- Note that some of the prompts already incorporate differentiation (in choice of prompt to answer or way of answering (label, describe, draw, etc.). Remind teachers that if writing is a problem for students, they need to find other ways to gather the information they are seeking.

Using Formative Assessment Data to Plan for Differentiation

Activity

Complete the following table using these guiding questions.

- Column 1: Study your assigned exit card or journal prompt.
- Column 2: Is the teacher is looking for information about student knowledge, understanding, or skill, or a combination of these? Be ready to justify your answer.
- Column 3: What range of answers should the teacher expect? What would indicate no, some, and sophisticated levels of knowledge, understanding, or skill?
- Column 4: Suppose the teacher gets a wide range of answers to the prompt. What might he or she do as a follow-up to ensure that all students have the opportunity to grow? Be specific.
- Anchor activity: If you finish before the others, complete at least one of the following:
    a. Use the last row of the table to devise and analyze an exit card or journal prompt that would work in your own classroom.
    b. Describe or suggest ways that the teacher might differentiate one of the prompts to meet varied readiness, interest, and/or learning profile needs.

Using Formative Assessment Data to Plan for Differentiation

Activity (Cont.)

Prompt or Assignment	Is the Teacher Measuring K, U, or D? (Explain your thinking)	What to Look for in Answers (the range of likely responses)	What Should Happen Next? (Ideas for follow-up differentiation)
Draw a picture to show what you learned about magnets from the experiment we did today.			
Write or draw three words you know that have a short vowel sound.			
List: 3 things you learned today 2 things you'd like to learn more about 1 question you still have			
We have been learning about the greenhouse effect. Define the term. Explain or diagram the importance of this issue to human survival. What questions do you have about this topic?			

Using Formative Assessment Data to Plan for Differentiation

Activity (Cont.)

Prompt or Assignment	Is the Teacher Measuring K, U, or D? (Explain your thinking)	What to Look for in Answers (the range of likely responses)	What Should Happen Next? (Ideas for follow-up differentiation)
Solve for *x*: 2*x* + 3 = 23 Name a real-life situation in which you might use an equation like this one.			
What does multiplication have to do with shopping?			
The muddiest point for me today is			
Choose one: • What does order of operations mean? Be sure to show that you know the correct order as part of your answer. • What might happen if there were no standard "order of operations"? Give a specific example. Be sure to show that you know the correct order as part of your answer.			

Part Three

Part Three

Using Formative Assessment Data to Plan for Differentiation

Activity (Cont.)

Prompt or Assignment	Is the Teacher Measuring K, U, or D? (Explain your thinking)	What to Look for in Answers (the range of likely responses)	What Should Happen Next? (Ideas for follow-up differentiation)
What are some tools we could use to measure?			
Why do historians use more than one source for information?			
What is the purpose of a hero in a story?			
Explain the difference between simile and metaphor. Give some examples of each as part of your explanation.			

Using Formative Assessment Data to Plan for Differentiation

Activity (Cont.)

Prompt or Assignment	Is the Teacher Measuring K, U, or D? (Explain your thinking)	What to Look for in Answers (the range of likely responses)	What Should Happen Next? (Ideas for follow-up differentiation)
We have been learning about plants. Draw a picture of a plant, and label its parts. Does every plant have these parts? Why or why not?			
Draw a clock that says 7:15.			
How is a tree like a person?			
In the story we are reading, who would you say is a good friend? Why?			

Part Three

Using Formative Assessment Data to Plan for Differentiation

Activity (Cont.)

Prompt or Assignment	Is the Teacher Measuring K, U, or D? (Explain your thinking)	What to Look for in Answers (the range of likely responses)	What Should Happen Next? (Ideas for follow-up differentiation)
What are dynamics? Why are they important? List examples you might see in a piece of music.			
Of the rights granted to you by the Constitution, which **one** right is most important to you? Why? What might make you change your mind about its importance?			
Is it ever OK for a musician to ignore dynamic markings? Explain your thinking.			
Write down De Morgan's Law. Why do programmers need to know this law?			

130

Using Formative Assessment Data to Plan for Differentiation

Activity (Cont.)

Prompt or Assignment	Is the Teacher Measuring K, U, or D? (Explain your thinking)	What to Look for in Answers (the range of likely responses)	What Should Happen Next? (Ideas for follow-up differentiation)
Draw and label the parts of a stage.			
Your friend just won a race. What Spanish phrase might you use to praise your friend?			
Based on what happened in today's game, what skill do you (or your team) most need to work on?			
What happens when you mix two primary colors? Give an example.			

Part Three

Part Three

Using Formative Assessment Data to Plan for Differentiation

Activity (Cont.)

Prompt or Assignment	Is the Teacher Measuring K, U, or D? (Explain your thinking)	What to Look for in Answers (the range of likely responses)	What Should Happen Next? (Ideas for follow-up differentiation)
Why does a town need firefighters and police officers?			
How is a swing set like a scientific experiment?			
What's one thing I could do to help you learn better?			
Check one: Today's lesson moved: ___ Too slowly for me. ___ At the right speed for me. ___ Too fast for me.			

Using Formative Assessment Data to Plan for Differentiation

Activity (Cont.)

Prompt or Assignment	Is the Teacher Measuring K, U, or D? (Explain your thinking)	What to Look for in Answers (the range of likely responses)	What Should Happen Next? (Ideas for follow-up differentiation)
My example:			

Part Three

Planning a Formative Assessment (Exit Card)

Rationale and Purpose

This tool offers teachers the opportunity to practice using exit cards as a strategy for ongoing assessment.

Directions

- Tell teachers: Just about anything students do over the course of a learning experience can be used as formative assessment data, including homework, quizzes, journal prompts, small-group discussions, exit cards, graphic organizers, and one-on-one conferences. (Note that pre-assessments are also a type of formative assessment since they inform the instruction that follows.) Remember, an activity is not a formative assessment if its main purpose is simply to fill up the grade book. It becomes a formative assessment only if the results will be used to alter what happens next for specific students. The keys to success with formative assessment in the differentiated classroom are:
  - Having a clear vision of what you want to find out;
  - Figuring out one or more ways to gather this information;
  - Interpreting the results; and
  - Adjusting follow-up instruction as necessary.
- Have teachers return to a KUD plan they wrote in an earlier activity or have used in the past.
- Working alone or with others who teach a similar unit, ask teachers to identify places in the unit where it would make sense to use an exit card to check the degree to which students have met unit objectives.
- Ask teachers to design an exit card that they could use to check for student knowledge, understanding, and/or skill.
- Remind teachers that exit cards should be designed so that they take only 3–5 minutes to complete at the end of the period. This is not the time for a lengthy essay.

Tips and Differentiation Options

- Allow teachers to work alone or with a partner who teaches a similar curriculum.
- Because teachers will be using the collected data to provide appropriate differentiation, suggest that they require students to put their names on their exit cards rather than answering anonymously.

What to Look For

- Don't let teachers begin to design an exit card (or other ongoing assessment) without first identifying what they want to find out about student knowledge, understanding, and/or skill.
- If teachers are still having trouble identifying whether they are checking for knowledge, understanding, or skill, revisit this concept with them or distribute the KUD References tool (available online only from www.ascd.org/downloads) before they begin.

Part Three

- One way to judge what is being measured is by the range of possible responses to the prompt. If there are only two possible responses—correct and incorrect—the prompt likely measures knowledge or skill. If there is a range of possible responses—novice, intermediate, advanced—then it likely measures understanding.
- Pay attention to the suggestions teachers make for follow-up differentiation. Make sure that the differentiated options lead to the same objective(s), are equally respectful, and help all students grow as much and as quickly as possible.
- Listen for teachers who are already thinking about ways to differentiate the prompts on their exit cards. This indicates that they not only understand the importance of formative assessment but also have internalized the varied readiness, interest, and learning profile needs evident in a differentiated classroom.

Part Three

Planning a Formative Assessment

Activity

In this activity, you will practice designing an appropriate exit card to use with students during the course of a unit of study.

Part 1: Define your vision.

Write your unit KUD statements below. Which aspects of your unit objectives do you want your exit card to focus on? Are you looking for information about knowledge? Understanding? Skill? A combination? Highlight or star those aspects of these areas that you will attempt to measure.

KNOW	UNDERSTAND	DO

Part 2: Design your prompt.

For this exercise, design an exit card prompt that measures aspects of your KUD goals.

Exit Card Prompt:

Challenge (optional): How might you differentiate the prompt to respond to key differences in your students' readiness, interest, and/or learning profile?

Variations:

Planning a Formative Assessment

Activity (Cont.)

Part 3: Interpret results.

What would an incorrect answer look like? A correct answer? A partially correct answer (if applicable)?

If you are measuring knowledge or skill:

Sample Correct Answer	Sample Incorrect Answer

If you are measuring understanding:

Answer Showing Novice/ Below-Grade-Level Understanding	Answer Showing Intermediate/ Grade-Level Understanding	Answer Showing Advanced/ Above-Grade-Level Understanding

Part 4: Use the results to differentiate.

Student's Current Level of Knowledge, Understanding, or Skill	Follow-Up Activity

Part Three

Differentiating a Summative Assessment

Rationale and Purpose

While it is quite possible to differentiate unit tests, many teachers are reluctant to do so because they worry about how to grade them. It is usually easier for teachers to think about ways to differentiate a performance assessment or final project for interest, readiness, and learning profile than it is to do so for a test. In this activity, teachers will examine performance tasks and think about ways to differentiate them.

Directions

- Display or distribute the sample performance task.
- Ask teachers to suggest ways to differentiate the task. Note:
  - Interest is already built into this task, since students can write to anyone about anything. If students have trouble thinking of someone to write to, the teacher might make a list of suggestions.
  - If the goal of the assessment is to write a letter, it doesn't seem appropriate to let students have a choice of the format in which they express their appreciation. However, graphic organizers might help students plan their letters. Some organizers could appeal to sequential thinkers, and others could be designed to appeal to more random thinkers. (If, on the other hand, the activity goal had been expressing appreciation, it would be perfectly acceptable to give students a choice of format, such as writing a letter, composing a thank-you song, or leaving a voicemail message.)
  - Some students will struggle with this task; others would not find it difficult at all. Readiness differentiation may be in order. Consider providing an outline or template for students who still have trouble writing letters to follow.
  - For students who need more of a challenge, change the task a bit: You must write a letter to someone who has done you a favor. Unfortunately, the favor did not turn out the way your friend expected. Write a thank-you letter that shows your appreciation but tactfully explains what happened as a result of that favor.
- Copy each remaining performance task onto a card. Hand out one card to each teacher or small group of teachers. Give each teacher a copy of the Differentiated Summative Assessment Template. Ask teachers to fill in the graphic organizer based on the performance task listed on their assigned card.

Tips and Differentiation Options

- At an earlier meeting or via e-mail, ask teachers to send you or bring you a project or performance task they have assigned in the past. Use these assignments as the starting point for this activity.

- You may hand out tasks at random or try to match teachers to tasks according to grade level or subject area.
- See McTighe and Wiggins (2004), pages 168–169, for additional performance assessment samples.

What to Look For

Teachers should provide respectful options that lead to the same outcome or KUD goals.

Part Three

Differentiating a Summative Assessment

Sample Performance Task Planner

Original Task:	When people do nice things for us, it is important to let them know that we appreciate their efforts. Your task is to write a letter to someone who has done something nice for you.
Possible KUD Goals:	**Know:** Parts of a friendly letter **Understand:** It is important to give reasons for our opinions. **Do:** Write a friendly letter

Thoughts About Differentiation:

Differentiating a Summative Assessment

Performance Tasks

Imagine that you are a personal trainer hired by the school district to help improve the fitness of district staff. Goals include weight reduction and improved muscle strength. Design a well-balanced 8-week program that will meet the staff's needs.

You must paint your house. Figure out the total volume of paint you need, as well as its cost.

You serve as a case worker at the psychiatric hospital where Holden Caulfield is telling his story. After a close reading and discussion of Holden's account of the events of the preceding December, write a letter to Holden's parents to describe Holden's behavior and explain what (if anything) is wrong with him. Cite examples from the text to support your analysis.

The local children's museum is looking for ideas on how to help children understand the impact of geography on culture. Make a detailed plan for a museum display to submit to the selection committee.

You have just returned from an adventure where you were unexpectedly dropped into a new environment. Back home, you wish to tell your classmates what happened to you and how you survived. Your job is to explain the resources of a particular habitat. Your work must show how humans meet their needs for shelter, food, water, and clothing in your assigned habitat. You may build a model of the environment that shows how you met your needs, write a series of letters about your experiences, or draw a series of illustrations for a picture book.

We need a new school song! Compose a song that is simple to play and expresses what is most important for people to know about our school.

Source: Task 3 adapted from *The Understanding by Design Professional Development Workbook* (p. 150), by J. McTighe and G. Wiggins, 2004, Alexandria, VA: ASCD. Copyright 2004 by ASCD.

Part Three

Differentiating a Summative Assessment

Activity

Directions:

- Use the sample performance task you are assigned or one of your own. Use the template on the next page to (1) identify the objective or KUD goals for the task and (2) brainstorm ideas for differentiating the tasks to meet varied student readiness, interest, and learning profile needs.

- Be ready to explain your thinking. Remember that if you differentiate the task, the resulting versions must still give you clear information on what the student knows, understands, or is able to do.

Considerations for Differentiation

- Who might need extra challenge? For these students, you could design a more sophisticated task or more complex challenge, a problem that is less well-defined, or a setting or context that is less familiar, or you could ask students to overcome more than one obstacle in accomplishing the task.

- Who might need extra support to be successful? Consider graphic organizers, templates, time lines, background information, vocabulary lists, technology support, and other resources. Design tasks that are more familiar, are well-defined, and have only one obstacle to overcome.

- To match your KUD goals, do all students have to play the same role? Could students choose or be assigned authentic roles that closely match their interests and learning profile? Do some roles require a more sophisticated understanding of content?

- Could you vary the audience students will target? For example, you could ask advanced students to present to a more sophisticated audience or use more complex tools or techniques. Some students may need more familiar audiences.

- What will students produce? Is there more than one product that would show student knowledge, understanding, and skill yet appeal to varied student interests and learning profile?

Differentiating a Summative Assessment

Activity (Cont.)

Differentiated Summative Assessment Template

Original Task:	
Possible KUD Goals:	Know: Understand: Do:
Thoughts About Differentiation:	

Part Three

Tools for Teachers

Part Three

Looking For Respect in All the Right Places
(Scenario Study)

Rationale and Purpose

This tool helps teachers recognize the difference between respectful and not-so-respectful differentiated activities.

Directions

- Place each scenario on a separate index card.
- Seat teachers in table groups of 6–8.
- Distribute one scenario at random to each pair of teachers. Ask them to read the scenario and discuss whether or not they think this is an example of respectful differentiation. If they do not think the example is respectful, they should suggest how to improve the situation.
- After 3–5 minutes, ask teachers to rotate cards and repeat with a new scenario. Complete as many rounds as practical.
- As a follow-up to this activity, ask each pair of teachers to join a second pair and complete one of the following activities:
    - Come up with a list of do's and don'ts for designing respectful differentiation.
    - Write your own pair of scenarios. One of the scenarios should represent differentiation that would not feel respectful to students. The other scenario should clearly fix the problems inherent in the first scenario.

Tips and Differentiation Options

- Use a different-colored card for each scenario. Laminate the cards for durability.
- Alternatively, leave the scenarios together, and distribute one copy to each teacher or pair of teachers. Assign or highlight the scenarios you wish them to consider.
- You could have participants compile the follow-up list of do's and don'ts as a whole-group.

What to Look For

- Scenario 1: It is not a good idea to differentiate for advanced students primarily by asking them to tutor other students. First of all, not all advanced students are good teachers! Sometimes they don't know *how* they know what they know. Some are not comfortable teaching their peers. The most important issue in this scenario, however, is that advanced students should also have an opportunity to expand their own knowledge, understanding, and skill with simple machines by completing more advanced activities.
- Scenario 2: Generally, it does not feel respectful to students when we differentiate by quantity rather than quality. While you do not need to have each version of an assignment be exactly the same length or cover exactly the same number of problems, too great a discrepancy will not seem fair to students.

                                                    147

Part Three

Rather than assigning fewer or more problems, assign *different* problems. A better solution in this scenario would be to assign everyone 10–12 problems at an appropriate level of difficulty. Struggling students would do problems that are simpler or more scaffolded; advanced students would skip those problems and move right to those that are more complex.

- Scenario 3: First of all, if most students get a choice of product, it would feel disrespectful to a single student to tell him that he does not get a choice. Furthermore, a good reason to offer choice in culminating products is so that students have the best possible chance to show their knowledge, understanding, and skill in a topic. The described student would be handicapped in this by having to do so in the medium that he finds most difficult.

- Scenario 4: This is a nice example of a teacher using pre-assessment results to eliminate aspects of the curriculum a student has already mastered. The alternative activity seems respectful. It should provide the student with an opportunity to refine his understanding of an effective PowerPoint presentation. His presentation to the class will inform his peers as well, providing them with access to advanced material.

- Scenario 5: Providing a choice of artistic periods is respectful. Human beings appreciate choice. What is not so respectful in this scenario is the assumption that ELL students should automatically be assigned the "simpler" version of the activity. The activity they are assigned should depend mainly on their readiness to accomplish the task itself (designing pop-up cards), not their ability to read the directions.

- Scenario 6: As in Scenario 2, this appears to be differentiation by quantity, not quality. If students cannot understand the whole chapter because of their reading level, they probably can't understand half the chapter, either! A better solution would be to adapt the reading selection to better match the varied reading levels in the class or to provide access to the material on tape.

- Scenario 7: Notice the similarity to Scenario 1. On the surface, this may seem a better use of student time than having them tutor their peers, and it certainly seems like an activity the students would enjoy. The problem is that it will seem like a small group of students gets a "fun" activity while the others are relegated to something that appears dull. Respectful differentiated activities are equally engaging.

- Scenario 8: This is another example of differentiation by quantity rather than quality. A better solution would be to assign advanced readers more advanced books or books that are in a less familiar genre.

- Scenario 9: On the surface this might not appear to be respectful because one student does not get as many choices as the other students. But in this case, the student finds too many choices overwhelming. Therefore, it seems appropriate to provide fewer options for this student, especially since the teacher has taken care to provide options he knows the student will enjoy.

- Scenario 10: Not every advanced student enjoys or is good at working on independent research. Furthermore, the differentiated activity appears to be unrelated to likely unit goals. Respectful differentiation leads students to the same—or very similar—KUD outcomes.

- Scenario 11: There are two problems with this scenario. First, we should not automatically assign a student to a particular level of a task based on a label. Perhaps these students have a greater background in music than she supposes. Some kind of pre-assessment would help the teacher more accurately assess this situation. Second, the goal of the task appears to have something to do with comparison of styles. If a student looks at only one composer, he cannot accomplish this goal.

- Scenario 12: Note the similarity to Scenario 6. However, in this situation, the teacher has adjusted the level of reading for her advanced students so they not only have access to key information but also have the opportunity to refine their decoding of advanced text. Another respectful aspect of this scenario is the use of the same set of discussion questions for all students, facilitating common discussions even if the texts differ.

Looking For Respect in All the Right Places

Scenarios

Scenario 1

Teacher A is helping students learn about simple machines and their uses in the real world. For most students, this is a fairly new topic. She does have a few students, however, who studied this in depth last year in the gifted pull-out class. When she assigns practice activities, she figures she will ask each experienced student to work in a small group with students who are new to the topic so that they can help those who are not as advanced in their knowledge of the topic. She figures that will help the advanced students, too, because students learn so much by teaching others.

Scenario 2

Teacher B is assigning math homework. Some of her students are still struggling to master converting fractions to decimals, some understand the process but need more practice, and some are fairly proficient. Because she knows that it will take longer for some students to complete the problems, she decides to assign 10 problems to struggling students, 20 problems to on-grade-level students, and 30 problems to advanced students.

Scenario 3

Teacher C likes to give students options when completing a culminating project in social studies. She typically tells them they can write a report, prepare a PowerPoint presentation, or give a speech that reveals their knowledge, understanding, and skill with a unit of study. However, one of her students is a really poor writer, so she asks him to do a report to give him additional practice with that skill.

Looking For Respect in All the Right Places

Scenarios (Cont.)

Scenario 4

Student D got a 100 on a pre-test that assessed his ability to use PowerPoint. So instead of the class demonstrations and assignments, his teacher asks him to design a rubric that he could use to judge the professional quality of a PowerPoint presentation. His task, over several days, is to use that rubric to evaluate several examples the teacher found on the Web. For fun, the teacher also throws in a presentation that she herself has designed. Student D must choose one of the examples and redo it so that it looks more professional. He will present both the "before" and "after" versions to the class.

Scenario 5

Teacher E is teaching his students to design pop-up cards that exemplify the style of different artistic movements. He has differentiated the assignment so that students can choose the two movements that most interest them. The methodology for the project is quite complex, so he designs a version of the assignment that is much simpler to complete. Because three students are non-English speakers, he assigns them to the simpler task.

Scenario 6

Teacher F is assigning a chapter in the science text. She knows that some students in her high school class read at an elementary level, some at a middle school level, some at grade level, and a few at a postsecondary level. But she only has one textbook. She tells students that she knows that some of them will have a hard time with the reading, but just to do as much of it as they can.

Looking For Respect in All the Right Places

Scenarios (Cont.)

Scenario 7

Teacher G is helping students learn about simple machines and their uses in the real world. A few students studied this in depth last year in an after-school enrichment class, but it is a fairly new topic for most students. Teacher G does not want to bore the experienced students with introductory lessons and worksheets, so he lets them work with building materials in the back of the room to construct a Rube Goldberg device that incorporates each type of simple machine at least once. The rest of the students will complete a packet of worksheets.

Scenario 8

Teacher H wants all students to complete outside reading. He asks each student to read 10 books per semester and record their reactions to the books in a journal. He provides a number of prompts to help them know what to write. Teacher H knows that a few students in his class read considerably above grade level, so he assigns them 20 books per semester.

Scenario 9

Teacher J likes to give students options when completing a culminating project. He typically tells them they can write a report, prepare a PowerPoint presentation, give a speech, design a Web page, write a skit, or design a series of posters. All work must meet a provided list of criteria. However, one of his students has a really hard time making choices, so he decides to limit this student's choices to three. He tries to pick three options that this student would find interesting.

Looking For Respect in All the Right Places

Scenarios (Cont.)

Scenario 10

One of Teacher K's students got a 100 on her word processing pre-test, so the teacher sends her to the library to do an independent research paper on the history of computers.

Scenario 11

Teacher L is assigning a project for which students will compare and contrast the musical styles of two composers of their choice. Two students in the class are classified as special education students, so she figures they will have trouble completing the fairly complex compare and contrast matrix she has designed. She assigns these students to study one composer, instead.

Scenario 12

Teacher M is assigning a reading in the psychology text on the multiple intelligence theories of Howard Gardner and Robert Sternberg. She has prepared questions for students to answer based on their reactions to the reading. She believes the reading level of the text is appropriate for most of her students, so she asks them to read the section in the text on this topic. However, a few students read and comprehend at a much higher level, so she gives them a reading on this topic from the AP text she has borrowed from her colleague down the hall.

ASCD®   153

Looking For Respect in All the Right Places

Activity

Directions:

- Read the assigned scenario.
- Discuss the scenario with your partner, and answer the following questions.

Scenario Number:

Is this an example of respectful differentiation? Why or why not?

How would you improve the assignment and adapt it for your class?

Part Three

Looking For Respect in All the Right Places

Activity (Cont.)

Scenario Number:

Is this an example of respectful differentiation? Why or why not?

How would you improve the assignment and adapt it for your class?

Evaluating Differentiated Activities

ACTION TOOL

Rationale and Purpose

An increasing amount of educational resources claim to provide differentiated activities. Some are of good quality, and some are of poor quality. Teachers need to become qualified consumers of differentiated materials. This tool helps them analyze their own and others' differentiated work for quality.

Directions

- Provide teachers with one of the sample differentiated activities provided (or another sample you have on hand) and a copy of the evaluation questions.
- Ask teachers to use the questions found in the tool to help them evaluate the quality of the differentiation in their example.
- If teachers are unhappy with an aspect of the activity they examine, they should suggest improvements.

Tips and Differentiation Options

- Before carrying out this activity, demonstrate how to analyze an activity for quality. Some teachers will need more guided practice than others. In that case, consider offering them the opportunity to work with you to analyze additional examples before branching out on their own.
- Some teachers will prefer to work alone; others prefer working with one or two colleagues. Allow them to make this choice.
- You may certainly hand out the differentiated activities at random, as teachers of all levels in all subject areas can learn from the work of teachers at all levels and in all subject areas. Some teachers find it easier to make the leap from disparate materials than others, however. For some groups, it may work better to give teachers activities that are at their grade levels or in their subject areas.
- If teachers have already designed some differentiated activities, encourage them to use the tool to evaluate and refine their own or one another's work.

What to Look For

Sample 1		Sample 2	
Pros	Cons	Pros	Cons
Teacher has identified goal of activity.	The options in the third column do not lead to the stated objective.	Use of all senses in both prompts promotes creativity.	The column on the right deals only with the canopy of the rain forest.

Sample 3		Sample 4	
Pros	Cons	Pros	Cons
Both require high-level thinking (evaluation) on the part of students.	Why not give the option of diagramming or modeling in option 2 as well?	Provides modeling for struggling group (basso). Scaffolding removed gradually as they move to alto and soprano groups.	To ensure high-level thinking, suggest that the teacher add the following question to columns 1 and 2: Why are these factors important in analyzing a composer's style?
Sample 5		**Sample 6**	
Pros	Cons	Pros	Cons
All activities appear to lead to same KUD objectives.	Only the practical version involves actually using the software. This may or may not be a concern.	All versions require that students provide evidence for their opinions.	We assume that communicating the world view of the characters is a goal of this activity, but the practical version does not require that students do so.
Sample 7		**Sample 8**	
Pros	Cons	Pros	Cons
Activity is nicely scaffolded.	Only the below-grade-level version offers a choice of products. If the teacher's goals for the activity include writing, then offering a choice of writing or speaking would be inappropriate.	Alien context may pique students' interest.	Hard to tell what the objective is for this activity. If writing is hard for some students, they may have difficulty communicating their knowledge via a lab report.
Sample 9		**Sample 10**	
Pros	Cons	Pros	Cons
Everyone gets to sort. Everyone works kinesthetically.	What if the advanced group does not sort according to vowel or consonant sounds? Is that a concern?	Task is differentiated for interest. There are lots of options to choose from. Students must justify their meal choices.	May need more specific criteria on what must be included in the meal. A rubric or checklist might help.

Part Three

Evaluating Differentiated Activities

Samples

Sample 1—Art: Choosing a Subject

Instructional goal: Understand how artists choose a subject for their work.

Prepare an oral explanation for a classmate of why your subject is important enough to paint.	Prepare a flowchart that illustrates how you go about choosing a subject or setting for your painting.	Make a soundscape (no words) that captures the same kind of feeling you wish your painting to capture.
Create a skit or pantomime that illustrates the right and the wrong way to go about choosing a subject for your work.	Find a quiet space, and write me a letter telling how you go about deciding on a subject for your painting. Let me inside your head!	Go outside to find inspiration for your painting. Sketch patterns, textures, and moods in nature that you wish to introduce into your work. How did this experience influence the final product?

Sample 2—Science

Instructional goal: Communicate knowledge about the rain forest.

Describe the rain forest using as much information as you can. Involve as many of your senses as possible in your description.	Describe how your life would change if you moved to the canopy of the rain forest, using as much information as you can about the canopy, involving as many of your senses as possible in your description, and explaining why these changes would take place.

Sample 3—Social Studies

Instructional goal: Describe the interaction of Native Americans and the early settlers.

Diagram or model the relationship between the early settlers and American Indians. Show the positives and negatives that came from that relationship.	Present an argument for or against the following: Did early settlers or American Indians benefit more from their relationship? Be sure to consider how someone taking the opposite position might respond as you prepare your most convincing argument.

Evaluating Differentiated Activities

Samples (Cont.)

Sample 4—Music Appreciation
Instructional goal: Compare the musical styles of Ives and Elgar.

Basso	Alto	Soprano
Using the provided grid, compare the musical styles of Ives and Elgar. Note that some cells are already filled in for you. Consider type of compositions, instrumentation, cultural influence, and at least one other variable.	Using the provided grid or another graphic organizer of your choice, compare the musical styles of Ives and Elgar. Consider type of compositions, instrumentation, cultural influence, and at least one other variable.	In a graphic organizer of your choice, compare and contrast the musical styles of Ives and Elgar. Include at least four important variables for comparison. Be ready to justify your choice of variables.

Sample 5—Computer-Aided Design
Instructional goal: Identify the capabilities and benefits of computer-aided design (CAD) software.

Practical	Creative	Analytical
Create and print a simple technical drawing using the CAD program. Label your drawing, and explain what command capabilities you used to make the drawing. Be ready to explain how specific tools work to simplify your task.	Write a paragraph telling how you would design an improved version of the CAD software you are using. Address drawing and command capabilities. Why would architects want to buy your "new and improved" version?	Write a paragraph explaining why the CAD drawing system results in faster and easier technical drawings. List several command capabilities, and explain why an architect would choose to use CAD programs instead of pencil techniques.

Sample 6—Literature (or Advanced French)
Instructional goal: Compare the perspectives of the two main characters in this novel.

Practical Prompt	Analytical Prompt	Creative Prompt
Why is it important that the Little Prince and the aviator understand each other's viewpoints?	In what ways are the Little Prince's and the aviator's worldviews similar and different?	How might the Little Prince's worldview be different if, like the aviator, he had lived his entire life on Earth?

Part Three

Evaluating Differentiated Activities

Samples (Cont.)

Sample 7—Math

Instructional goal: Design, carry out, and share the results of a survey.

Below Grade	On Grade	Above Grade
Design a survey to distribute to your classmates. Follow the steps below: 1. Write your question. 2. Design four likely answers to the question. 3. Distribute your survey. 4. Based on the results, fill out the provided frequency table. 5. Place the results into a bar graph or pie chart format. (You may ask your teacher for sample graphs.) 6. Write a brief summary **or** prepare an oral presentation that communicates the results of your survey and answers the following questions: What was your question? Who did you ask? What were the results?	Design a survey to distribute to your classmates. Follow the steps below. 1. Write your question. 2. Design four likely answers to the question. 3. Distribute your survey. 4. Design a frequency table to help you tabulate the results. 5. Place the results into an appropriate graph. 6. Write a brief summary of the results of your survey for publication in the school newspaper.	Design a survey to distribute to your classmates. Follow the steps below: 1. Write your question. 2. Design four or five likely answers to the question. 3. Distribute your survey. 4. Compile your data using an appropriate frequency table. 5. Choose a graph design that would best communicate the data you collected. Be ready to explain why you chose the type of graph you did and why your choice was a good one. 6. Write an analysis of your survey as if it were an article for a math journal. What was your question? Who did you ask? What were the results? What are possible sources of error? What are the real-world implications for your findings?

Sample 8—Biology

Instructional goal: Describe the parts of a cell and how they support the work of the cell.

You have been hit by an alien ray and have been shrunk small enough to travel through the bloodstream. Write a narrative or a play to describe what you see as you come upon a specific cell and what happens to you once you get inside the plasma membrane.	You are a scientist working in New Mexico when a spaceship crashes. You are charged with figuring out the biology of the alien species that was in the spaceship. You do some preliminary research and find that this alien has something similar to cells, just like Earth's organisms. Compare and contrast all of the Earth's organism's organelles with the alien species'. Write a lab report on your findings.

Evaluating Differentiated Activities

Samples (Cont.)

Sample 9—Reading

Instructional goal: Given a set of words or picture cards, sort according to similar attributes.

Novice	Intermediate	Advanced
Sort the cards into two piles: Pile 1 is for words that begin with consonants, and pile 2 is for words that begin with vowels.	Sort the cards into two piles: Pile 1 is for words with long vowels, and pile 2 is for words with short vowels.	Sort the cards into two piles. Be ready to explain why you sorted them the way you did.

Sample 10—Nutrition

Instructional goal: Plan a healthy menu.

> You are planning a party. Decide who the party is for and when and where it will take place. Then design a healthy, balanced menu for the party. Be ready to explain your choices.

Part Three

 161

Evaluating Differentiated Activities

Activity

Use the following questions to help you evaluate sample differentiated activities:

1. What makes this high-quality or poor-quality curriculum?

2. How does each version of the task appear to lead to the same goals (KUD)? If this isn't true, what changes need to be made to ensure that each task supports the KUD goals?

3. How are the differentiated tasks equally respectful?
   a. Is each version equally engaging from the perspective of the students it's designed for? If not, what changes could be made to ensure equal engagement?

   b. Does each version require students to stretch as much as possible? If not, what changes could be made to ensure that each task is equally challenging?

Planning a Tiered Activity

Rationale and Purpose

This tool provides teachers with a format for planning tiered activities, which are designed to help students at different levels of readiness meet common KUD goals.

Directions

- Review the definition and purposes of tiered activities.
- Distribute a copy of the tool to each teacher. Tell them they will use the tool to help them design an activity that is differentiated for student readiness.
- Tell teachers they may skip Step 2 if they wish.
- Point out that Step 3 of the planner asks teachers to begin by designing an activity that would challenge their most advanced students. This may differ from how they usually plan, but encourage them to try it. When teachers plan this way, they often find that they have raised the challenge level for all students while providing appropriate scaffolding.
- Remind teachers that they are not limited to three tiers. For a particular set of objectives or a particular set of students, two or four tiers may be more appropriate.
- Ask teachers to share their work with another teacher or group of teachers to give and receive feedback on their work.

Tips and Differentiation Options

- Some teachers will work better on their own; others will prefer to work with colleagues who teach the same or a similar curriculum. Allow them to choose.
- If teachers prefer to use a different format for their planning, let them. The format doesn't matter as much as ensuring that they begin with identifying their objectives and that these objectives include Understand goals or the equivalent.
- Novice differentiators will probably find it easier to differentiate an activity in a familiar area of the curriculum that they particularly enjoy teaching, especially if the activity has been successful in the past.
- Suggest that teachers who have experience with differentiation try to plan a differentiated activity in a subject or topic area that is less familiar to them.
- Step 2 is optional. This step is a helpful start for some teachers, but it may lock others into a preconceived way of designing the activity. Watch for this, and make appropriate changes to the planner.
- If possible, collect the work to analyze it and give feedback.

Part Three

What to Look For

- Check that teachers have identified an appropriate KUD plan and that any understandings truly represent "big ideas."
- Make sure that each version of the activity leads students to increased competency with activity goals.
- Make sure that each version of the activity will feel respectful to students.

Part Three

Planning a Tiered Activity

Activity

Step 1: Devise KUD goals (what you want students to know, understand, and be able to do as a result of the lesson or activity).

KNOW (facts, dates, definitions, rules, people, places)	UNDERSTAND (big ideas, principles, generalizations, rules, the "point" of the discipline or topic within the discipline) *I want students to understand that . . .*	BE ABLE TO DO (skills of literacy, numeracy, communication, thinking, planning, production, etc.; start with a verb such as: describe, explain, show, compare, synthesize, analyze, apply, construct, or solve)

Step 2: Determine your usual starting point (optional).

Jot down what you would typically do in this lesson if you were **not** going to differentiate. (Sketch out the steps you would follow or the assignment you would give.)

Planning a Tiered Activity

Activity (Cont.)

Step 3: Write differentiated plans.

Think about the most advanced student you have ever had. Design an activity (clearly related to your KUD goals) that would stretch this student.	Figure out ways to scaffold the task so that students at or near grade level can be successful with the task. Make sure this version still matches your KUD goals.	Figure out ways to further scaffold the task so that students who may struggle with the task can be successful. Double-check that you have not watered down the task to the point that students miss out on the KUD goals.

Step 4: Check your KUD goals.
- Double-check that every version of the activity leads students to increased competency with activity goals. If not, adjust as needed.
- Double-check that every version of the activity will feel respectful to the student for whom it is designed. If not, adjust as needed.

Part Three

Planning a Tiered Activity

Activity (Cont.)

Step 5: Assess your plans.

- Where might you run into trouble in carrying out the differentiation in this lesson?

- How will you give directions for each version of the task? Will you color-code task cards or assignment sheets? Audio-record directions?

- Will you tell students the lesson is differentiated? If so, how? If not, why not?

- What will you do if some students or groups finish early?

- If necessary, how will you get students into groups efficiently? How will you get them back to a whole-class configuration?

Part Three

Part Three

Planning a Differentiated Activity

ACTION TOOL

Rationale and Purpose

The Planning a Tiered Activity tool (p. 163) focused on differentiation for readiness. This tool provides a template for planning activities that are differentiated for student interest, learning profile, or readiness.

Directions

- Review the characteristics of a high-quality differentiated activity.
- Distribute a copy of the activity planner to each teacher.
- Remind teachers that they are not limited to three versions of the activity. For a particular set of objectives or a particular set of students, a different number of versions may be more appropriate.
- Ask teachers to share their work with another teacher or group of teachers to give and receive feedback on their work.

Tips and Differentiation Options

- Some teachers will work better on their own; others will prefer to work with colleagues who teach the same or a similar curriculum. Allow them to choose.
- If teachers prefer to use a different format for their planning, let them. The format doesn't matter as much as ensuring that they begin with identifying their objectives and that these objectives include Understand goals or the equivalent.
- Novice differentiators will probably find it easier to differentiate an activity in a familiar area of the curriculum that they particularly enjoy teaching, especially if the activity has been successful in the past.
- Suggest that teachers who have experience with differentiation try to plan a differentiated activity in a subject or topic area that is less familiar to them.
- Step 2 is optional. This step is a helpful start for some teachers, but it may lock others into a preconceived way of designing the activity. Watch for this, and make appropriate changes to the planner.
- If possible, collect the work to analyze it and give feedback.

What to Look For

- Check to be sure that teachers have identified an appropriate KUD plan and that any understandings represent "big ideas."
- Make sure that each version of the activity will feel respectful to students.
- Make sure that each version of the activity leads students to increased competency with activity goals.

Planning a Differentiated Activity

Activity

Step 1: Devise KUD goals (what you want students to know, understand, and be able to do as a result of the lesson or activity).

KNOW (facts, dates, definitions, rules, people, places)	UNDERSTAND (big ideas, principles, generalizations, rules, the "point" of the discipline or topic within the discipline) *I want students to understand that . . .*	BE ABLE TO DO (skills of literacy, numeracy, communication, thinking, planning, production, etc.; start with a verb such as: describe, explain, show, compare, synthesize, analyze, apply, construct, or solve)

Step 2: Determine your usual starting point (optional).

Jot down what you would typically do in this lesson if you were **not** going to differentiate. (Sketch out the steps you would follow or the assignment you would give.)

ASCD® © 2009 ASCD. All Rights Reserved.

Part Three

Planning a Differentiated Activity

Activity (Cont.)

Step 3: Write differentiated plans.
- Think about the students for whom you are planning this activity. What kind of differentiation would best meet their needs? Readiness? Interest? Learning profile?
- Next, decide how many variations of the activity you should have to meet these needs. Be reasonable!
- Use the space below to outline the various versions of the activity.

Version 1	Version 2
Version 3	**Version 4**

Step 4: Check your KUD goals.
- Double-check that every version of the activity will feel respectful to the student for whom it is designed. If not, adjust as needed.
- Double-check that every version of the activity leads students to increased competency with activity goals. If not, adjust as needed.

Planning a Differentiated Activity

Activity (Cont.)

Step 5: Assess your plans.

- Where might you run into trouble in carrying out the differentiation in this lesson?

- How will you give directions for each version of the task? Will you color-code task cards or assignment sheets? Audio-record directions?

- Will you tell students the lesson is differentiated? If so, how? If not, why not?

Planning a Differentiated Activity

Activity (Cont.)

- What will you do if some students or groups finish early?

- If necessary, how will you get students into groups efficiently? How will you get them back to a whole-class configuration?

- How will you know if today's lesson "worked"? What will you watch for? How will you use what happens in this lesson to improve the next day's instruction?

Part Three

Sharing Your Differentiated Activity

Rationale and Purpose

This tool provides a list of discussion questions that teachers can use when sharing their work with colleagues.

Directions

- Divide teachers into small groups of 3–4, and give each teacher a copy of the tool.
- Explain that teachers will each take a turn to share their differentiated activities, using the provided questions as a reference for their commentaries. Tell them how long each teacher will have to share his or her work. Encourage teachers to solicit suggestions from the small group once they have finished their presentations.
- As a large group, ask each teacher or group of teachers to share an insight they gained from sharing their differentiated activities.

Tips and Differentiation Options

- Place the questions on a card, and laminate for later use. These questions will work with any differentiated activity.
- This activity works well in groups with as few as 2 people and as many as 5–6.
- If possible, ask teachers to bring enough copies of their tasks for each teacher in their small group.
- It generally works best to have teachers share with others in their own subject area or grade level. If this is not possible, try to group them so they are in similar school levels (primary, upper elementary, middle, high).
- Try to have a mixture of newer and more experienced teachers in each group.
- Appoint or ask each group to appoint a discussion leader and a timer to help them stay on track. This models an effective classroom practice with students.
- Teachers asked to present at a faculty meeting or staff development session can use the questions in this tool as a preplanning aid.

What to Look For

- Circulate as teachers discuss. Listen for indicators of the degree to which teachers:
  - Thought carefully about what was being differentiated and why.
  - Analyzed the success of implementation.
  - Reflected on ways to improve the activity and their own next steps for growth in differentiation.
- Listen for teachers who are particularly good at expressing themselves with peers. Consider asking them to present other differentiated activities they try to the whole group at a later date.

Sharing Your Differentiated Activity

Activity

You will each share a differentiated activity that you have designed and carried out. If possible, provide each member of your group with a copy of your differentiated activity or lesson plan. Before sharing, jot down your thoughts about the following questions, and use them to frame your explanation of the activity.

What were your objectives for this activity?

Why did you feel the need to differentiate this activity?

How did you decide the kind of differentiation to use (readiness, interest, learning profile)? In retrospect, was this a good choice? Why?

How did you decide on the number of versions? In retrospect, was this a good choice? Why?

What made each version of your activity equally engaging and challenging?

How did you decide who got which version? Did you make the right choices? Why?

Sharing Your Differentiated Activity

Activity (Cont.)

What was the level of quality of student work? Did some versions yield better work than others? If so, what changes would you make to the activity?

Did you tell students that the activity was differentiated? Why or why not? Was this a good choice? Why?

Part Three

How did you handle the management issues (giving multiple directions, rearranging the room, distributing materials, dealing with early finishers, etc.)?

What other changes would you make to the activity if you could do it again?

What will you try next to further your growth in differentiated practices?

Differentiation Strategies Jigsaw

ACTION TOOL

Rationale and Purpose

This tool offers an efficient way to introduce teachers to a number of strategies that are useful in the differentiated classroom.

Directions

Before the jigsaw:

- Prepare packets for each targeted strategy that include a brief overview of the strategy along with examples at a variety of grade levels and in a variety of subject areas. You can find examples of these and other strategies in *Tools for High-Quality Differentiated Instruction: An ASCD Action Tool* (Strickland, 2007) and the *Differentiation in Practice* books (Tomlinson & Eidson, 2003a, 2003b; Tomlinson & Strickland, 2005).
- Ask teachers to form groups of 4.
- Distribute the jigsaw directions and the graphic organizer. Carefully go over the directions, highlighting the discussion items in parts 2 and 4.
- Assign a particular area of the room to each strategy. For ease of distribution, have the materials teachers will need already at each location. If the group is large, you may need more than one specialty group per strategy.
- Once teachers have chosen their specialty strategy, direct them to the part of the room devoted to that strategy. Distribute the appropriate packet to each teacher.

During the jigsaw:

- Set a timer to remind you and the teachers when it is time to move onto the next part of the jigsaw. Regroup as directed.
- It is vital that you check in with every specialty group at least once during their discussion to answer questions and check for understanding. You don't want "experts" to misinform their home groups!

After the jigsaw, meet as a whole group to debrief. Ask:

- What questions do you still have about the strategies you studied?
- What do these strategies all have in common? How do they fit into the differentiation model? Which strategies are you most likely to use? Why?
- Discuss the jigsaw strategy. What is it? How does it work? What is the teacher's role in setting up a successful jigsaw? The student's role?

Tips and Differentiation Options

- Assign the following exit card: Choose one of the strategies you learned about today. State one specific way you might use that strategy in your own classroom.
- If you have access to the ASCD *Instructional Strategies for the Differentiated Classroom* videos and the space to set up several viewing stations, consider playing excerpts from the matching video at each station or offering the option of watching the video instead of reading the packet of materials. The instructional guides that accompany these videos have sample lessons that you can copy and distribute to viewers.
- Feel free to change strategies depending on the examples you have available or the grade level of the teachers you are working with.
- The time frame for each step is only a suggestion. Use your judgment.
- This jigsaw works well with up to six strategies (six teachers per group).
- This jigsaw is loosely differentiated for teacher interest (teachers negotiate specialty areas as a small group). To refine the match between strategy and teacher, ask them at a prior staff development session to rank their interest in the various strategies to be presented. Use that information to assign teachers to specialty areas. You will need to balance the number of teachers assigned to each strategy so you can form home groups that represent each of the strategies.
- Steer teachers who are new to differentiation toward those strategies that are a bit less complex (e.g., RAFT versus contracts; tiered questioning versus tiered activities).
- Encourage teachers with more experience with differentiation to try a strategy that is new to them or that is more complex.
- If your time is limited or you wish simply to introduce the strategies, you may chose to skip the work group (Step 3). However, many teachers appreciate the opportunity to design something to use in their own classroom.

What to Look For

- Accurate interpretation of the strategies and their role in the differentiated classroom.
- Teacher examples that accurately apply the strategies, exemplifying variations that lead to the same KUD goals and are equally respectful.
- Realization that not all strategies work in all situations
- Realization that most strategies can be adapted for use in the differentiated classroom and most lessons can be differentiated in more than one way. The kind of differentiation teachers choose depends on
  - Curricular goals.
  - Characteristics and needs of students for whom the activity is designed.
  - Teacher's comfort level with a particular strategy.

Differentiation Strategies Jigsaw

Activity

Directions:

1. Form a home group.
   - You may wish to work with others who teach at your grade level or in your subject area. The ideal group size is 4.
   - Assign each member of your home group to one of the four strategies listed below. (Cover all of the strategies, if you can.)
     - RAFT: Strategy where the student is asked to take on a Role, speaking to a particular Audience, in a given Format, and on a specific Topic.
     - Learning Menus or Contracts: Students have choice in some tasks, the length of time they work on individual tasks, and the order in which they complete them.
     - Cubing or ThinkDots: Originally based on Bloom's taxonomy; students respond to multiple prompts in a game format to look at content from several perspectives.
     - Sternberg Intelligences: Based on Robert Sternberg's work in multiple intelligences; students work on one of three intelligence-based tasks: analytical, practical, or creative.

2. Meet in specialty study groups.

   Part 1 *(about 15 minutes)*
   - When the signal is given, move to the area of the room corresponding to the strategy you have been assigned.
   - Working alone, read the materials provided, and study the various examples. Remember that you can learn from examples at all levels and in all subject areas.
   - Place a sticky note on one or two of the examples that you especially like. Jot down any questions you have about the strategy.

   Part 2 *(about 15 minutes)*
   - Discuss the strategy in your large specialty group. As you discuss, fill out the appropriate row in your graphic organizer. Appoint a discussion leader who will use the questions below as a discussion guide:
     - What is this strategy? How does it work?
     - What is the intent or purpose of this strategy? What kind(s) of differentiation does the strategy target?
     - What are the particular strengths and weaknesses of this strategy?
     - What management suggestions do you have for implementing this strategy?

   Note: All individuals should go away from the discussion confident in their ability to (1) effectively teach the strategy to their home groups, and (2) answer questions about the use of the strategy.

Differentiation Strategies Jigsaw

Activity (Cont.)

3. Form work groups. *(about 30 minutes)*
   - Now, subdivide your specialty group into work groups of 1–3 people.
   - Each work group should create an original application of the strategy for an agreed-upon grade level and subject.
   - Make sure the first step in designing the application is to write out the learning goal for the activity. This is to ensure that all versions of your activity lead to the same goal. Challenge: Do this in the KUD format. (See below for help.)

     KNOW:

     Facts, names, dates, places, information, definitions

     UNDERSTAND:

     Essential truths that give meaning to the topic; stated as a full sentence. Begin with "I want students to understand *that* . . ." (not *how* or *why*).

     BE ABLE TO DO:

     Skills (basic skills, skills of the discipline, skills of independence, social skills, skills of production)

   - You will each be sharing this example with your home group, so be sure everyone in the work group walks away with his or her own copy of the application.

4. Return to your home group. *(about 45 minutes)*
   - For each of the four strategies, devote 7–8 minutes (appoint a timer!) to:
     - Explaining, discussing, and critiquing the strategy.
     - Sharing a favorite example from the strategy booklet. (Remember, you marked good ones with sticky notes.)
     - Sharing the example you created in your work group.
   - Each group member should use the graphic organizer to record notes and thoughts about each of the strategies.
   - Anchor activity if you finish early: Discuss the jigsaw strategy that you have just experienced, and fill out the corresponding jigsaw row on the graphic organizer.

Part Three

ASCD® 179

Differentiation Strategies Jigsaw

Activity (Cont.)

Strategy	What Is It? (description)	Why Use It? (purpose, advantages)	Considerations (worries, cautions, management tips)
RAFTs			
Learning Menus/Contracts			
Cubing/ThinkDots			
Sternberg Intelligences			
Anchor Row: Jigsaws			

Tools for Teachers

Part Three

Incorporating Flexible Grouping into Unit Design (Novice)

Rationale and Purpose

Teachers new to differentiation will typically begin their journeys by focusing on student interest **or** learning profile **or** readiness. Different teachers will be drawn to different aspects of student differences. Each of those points is a good place to start, but over time, teachers need to become comfortable with all aspects of differentiation. The goal of this activity is to help teachers add to their differentiation repertoires and expand their comfort levels with differentiating for interest, learning profile, and readiness.

Directions

- Before the session, inform teachers that they will need to bring planning materials for a specific unit of study to this workshop.
- Share the Key Questions in Planning a Differentiated Unit. Tell teachers that in this exercise they will focus on Question 5, which revolves around the concept of flexible grouping.
- Ask teachers to think about the balance of differentiation opportunities that they have provided students over the past year. Tell them this session will give them the opportunity to design differentiation in an area in which they are less experienced or have focused less time so far. In other words, if they find they have not done much differentiating for learning profile, they should concentrate on that area for this activity.
- Distribute the tool, and ask teachers to follow the instructions.
- Ask teachers to share their work with another teacher or group of teachers to give and receive feedback on their work.
- If possible, collect the work to analyze it and give feedback.

Tips and Differentiation Options

- If necessary, remind teachers of what good differentiation for interest, for learning profile, and for readiness looks like. Provide examples for those who need them.
- Ask teachers to differentiate a new aspect of their unit **or** adapt a current activity that they have differentiated for one of the factors so that it responds to student variation in the other two areas, instead.
- Ask teachers to add a second layer of differentiation to their current activities. For example, if they have differentiated an activity for analytical, practical, and creative intelligences, have them come up with a second version of each activity that is at a more or less advanced readiness level.
- Distribute the Student Variance Reminder Cards (available online only from www.ascd.org/downloads) to those who need them.

- You may use this tool with the intermediate and advanced variations (pp. 187, 199) by distributing the appropriate variation to each teacher.

What to Look For

- Watch for teachers who are struggling with one or more aspects of differentiation so that you can provide the support or coaching they need.
- If you notice that any teachers have a fairly even balance of differentiation for interest, learning profile, and readiness, you may wish to ask them to complete the intermediate version (p. 187) instead.

Incorporating Flexible Grouping into Unit Design (Novice)

Key Questions in Planning a Differentiated Unit

1. What are my *unit* objectives?

2. Do I need to differentiate this unit?

3. If so, when and where would work best (both for me and for my students)?

4. How can I ensure that my differentiation is respectful?

5. Over time, are my differentiated practices *balanced*? Do I use a variety of differentiation techniques, including flexible grouping?

Part Three

Incorporating Flexible Grouping into Unit Design (Novice)

Activity

1. Think about the past semester or school year. What differentiation options have you offered students during this time? Label each instance as primarily responding to differences in student interests (I), learning profile (LP), or readiness (R).

2. Most of us tend to emphasize one type of differentiation over another, especially at the early stages of learning about differentiation. Using your list, examine the degree to which your differentiation has been balanced over time.

3. Choose the area of student variance to which you have responded the least often, and design an activity that is differentiated for that aspect. Be sure you start with a KUD plan, using the template below.

Activity:

Student Variance Area:

KNOW	UNDERSTAND	BE ABLE TO DO

Part Three

Incorporating Flexible Grouping into Unit Design (Intermediate)

ACTION TOOL

Rationale and Purpose

As teachers become more comfortable with differentiation, they should be encouraged to incorporate more than one aspect of differentiation into their unit plans. This activity is suitable for teachers who have a basic understanding of differentiation and have investigated several differentiated strategies.

Directions

- Before the session, inform teachers that they will need to bring planning materials for a specific unit of study to this workshop.
- Share the Key Questions in Planning a Differentiated Unit (p. 185). Tell teachers that this in this exercise they will focus on Question 5, which revolves around the concept of flexible grouping.
- Distribute a copy of the tool (or parts of the tool; see below) to each teacher. Tell teachers that the goal of this activity is to help them increase the amount and kind of differentiation they offer over time in their classrooms. Tell them they will use this tool to brainstorm places in a unit of study where it would make sense to differentiate for interest, for learning profile, and for readiness.
- Ask teachers to share their work with another teacher or group of teachers to give and receive feedback on their work.
- If possible, collect the work to analyze it and give feedback.

Tips and Differentiation Options

- If necessary, remind teachers of what good differentiation for interest, for learning profile, and for readiness looks like. Provide examples for those who need them.
- If you are pressed for time, have everyone focus on only one aspect of learning profile or one aspect of readiness. In that case, hand out only the pertinent parts of the tool.
- In the spirit of teacher growth, encourage teachers to expand their repertoires. Encourage teachers who already differentiate for learning styles, for example, to focus on a different aspect of learning profile. The more ways teachers have of thinking about learning profile, the more likely they are to meet students' needs and provide opportunities for students to work with a variety of peers.
- You may use this tool with the novice and advanced versions (pp. 183, 199) by distributing the appropriate variation to each teacher.

What to Look For

- Watch for teachers who are struggling with one or more aspects of differentiation so that you can provide the support or coaching they need.

- Ensure that teachers move on to the sections of the planner that focus on *differentiating* for interest and learning profile rather than simply *responding*. It is good teaching to provide overall variety in a unit of study, but teaching is differentiated only when there are multiple versions of an activity, leading to the same goals, but assigned or chosen according to specific student needs.
- Teachers who are coming up with multiple ideas for differentiation by interest, learning profile, and readiness may be ready for more advanced attention to flexible grouping. Suggest they try the advanced version of the tool (p. 199).

Incorporating Flexible Grouping into Unit Design (Intermediate)

Differentiating for Student Interest (1)

Sometimes the same objectives can be met through a variety of interest lenses. Consider the various aspects or parts of your unit topics. Where in the unit might it make sense to offer students a choice of topic, perspective, area of specialization, or focus? Sketch out an idea or two below.

Idea 1:

Idea 2:

Incorporating Flexible Grouping into Unit Design (Intermediate)

Differentiate for Student Interest (2)

Anchor activities, which students are taught to turn to when they finish early or are waiting for teacher help, are a perfect way to weave student interests into unit activities. They are differentiated because students have a choice of activity to complete.

Use your knowledge of student interests and the template below to plan anchor activities that you could use in your classroom. Remember, the best anchor activities are related to unit or subject goals, are highly interesting to students, and can be completed independently.

Activity 1:
Activity 2:
Activity 3:

Incorporating Flexible Grouping into Unit Design (Intermediate)

Differentiate for Learning Profile

When could you provide more than one way for students to access unit content, make sense of that content, or show what they have learned? When would it make most sense to let students indulge their learning preferences? When might it make sense to ask them to stretch by working in a way that is less familiar or less comfortable?

Note that it is also possible to ask some students to work in their preferred modality and ask others to stretch. If the work is particularly challenging for a student, it would be better for him or her to work in a preferred modality. You might ask students who find the work less rigorous to stretch. Choose from the following templates to help you differentiate for student learning profile.

Aspect 1: Grouping Options

Design activities in which students could choose whether to work alone (A), with a partner (P), or in small groups (SG).

Activity	Appropriate Grouping Options

Incorporating Flexible Grouping into Unit Design (Intermediate)

Differentiate for Learning Profile (Cont.)

Aspect 2: Learning Styles

Design versions of an activity in which students could choose (or be asked) to work primarily in visual (learn through seeing), auditory (learn through listening), or kinesthetic (learn through moving, doing, and touching) modalities. Indicate whether students will work in a preferred modality (P) or be asked to stretch (S).

Visual Version	Auditory Version	Kinesthetic Version

Aspect 3: Sternberg Intelligence Preferences

Sternberg and Grigorenko (2007) identify three types of thinkers:

- Analytic thinkers use conscious direction of mental processes to find a thoughtful solution to a problem, are able to think critically, and prefer analyzing, judging, critiquing, and comparing.
- Practical thinkers are able to translate theory into practice and abstract ideas into practical accomplishments, prefer applying or using what they learn, and recognize ideas that have a potential audience.
- Creative thinkers are able to generate novel and interesting ideas and prefer creating, discovering, and inventing.

Design versions of an activity in which students could choose (or be asked) to work analytically, practically, or creatively.

Analytic Version	Practical Version	Creative Version

Incorporating Flexible Grouping into Unit Design (Intermediate)

Differentiate for Learning Profile (Cont.)

Aspect 4: Preference for Competition or Collaboration

Design versions of an activity in which students could choose (or be asked) to compete against others, compete against themselves, or collaborate instead of compete.

Compete Against Others	Compete Against Self	Collaborate Instead of Compete

Aspect 5: Extrovert or Introvert

- Extroverts draw energy from the outside world of people, activities, things; prefer interaction with others; are action oriented; and prefer to recharge their batteries in the company of others.
- Introverts draw energy from their internal world of ideas, emotions, impressions; prefer reflecting and concentrating; and prefer to recharge their batteries alone or with one other person.

Design versions of an activity in which students could choose (or be asked) to work in a way that is comfortable for an extrovert or an introvert.

Extrovert Version	Introvert Version

Incorporating Flexible Grouping into Unit Design (Intermediate)

Considering and Responding to Differences in Student Readiness

In what ways do your students vary the most? How might you respond? Choose one or more of the following, and sketch out differentiation ideas.

Aspect 1: Prerequisite Skills

Prerequisite skills students will need to be successful in this unit:	Ways I might accommodate students with **learning gaps** and teach them the needed skills (graphic organizers, vocabulary lists, minilessons, etc):

Part Three

Incorporating Flexible Grouping into Unit Design (Intermediate)

Considering and Responding to Differences in Student Readiness (Cont.)

Aspect 2: Reading Level

Points in the unit when a student's **reading level** may be an issue:	Ways I will support students who will **struggle** with the reading:	Ways I could stretch **advanced** readers:

Part Three

Incorporating Flexible Grouping into Unit Design (Intermediate)

Considering and Responding to Differences in Student Readiness (Cont.)

Aspect 3: Prior Knowledge, Understanding, or Skill

For students I suspect already have a significant body of knowledge, understanding, or skill in unit topics:	
What I will do to **ensure** that I have appropriate evidence of that knowledge, understanding, and skill:	What I will do to ensure that these students also have an opportunity to **learn and grow** during the unit:

Part Three

Incorporating Flexible Grouping into Unit Design (Intermediate)

Considering and Responding to Differences in Student Readiness (Cont.)

Aspect 4: Speed of Learning

What I will do to ensure that students who are likely to master unit knowledge, understanding, and skill more quickly than their peers don't have to wait for others to catch up but can continue their learning or refine their understanding and skill to more expert levels:

Part Three

Incorporating Flexible Grouping into Unit Design (Intermediate)

Considering and Responding to Differences in Student Readiness (Cont.)

Other Aspects

Consider other ways that your students vary significantly in terms of readiness (e.g., small- or large-motor skills, attention issues, writing ability, reasoning and thinking skills, communication skills, group-work skills, resources at home, research skills, computer skills, IEP issues, language skills, gifted identification).

Issue	Response (Consider and adjust for both deficits and particular strengths in these areas.)

Incorporating Flexible Grouping into Unit Design (Advanced)

Rationale and Purpose

This activity is suitable for teachers who have a sophisticated understanding of differentiation and wish to refine their flexible grouping practices. They will consider differentiation not only for readiness, interest, and learning profile but also of content, process, and product.

Directions

- Before the session, inform teachers that they will need to bring planning materials for a specific unit of study to this workshop.
- Distribute a copy of the tool to each teacher.
- Tell teachers that the goal of this activity is to help them increase the amount and kind of differentiation they offer over time in their classroom. This tool will help them investigate a myriad of ways to differentiate the content, processes, and products of a unit for interest, learning profile, and readiness.
- Ask teachers to share their work with another teacher or group of teachers to give and receive feedback on their work.
- If possible, collect the work to analyze it and give feedback.

Tips and Differentiation Options

- If needed, provide a brief refresher of the definitions of *content*, *process*, and *product* and *interest*, *readiness*, and *learning profile*.
- Remind teachers that the sample grid is suggestive rather than exhaustive of possibilities for differentiation.
- You may use this tool with the novice and intermediate versions (pp. 183, 187) by distributing the appropriate variation to each teacher.

What to Look For

- Watch for teachers who are struggling with one or more aspects of differentiation so that you can provide the support or coaching they need.
- Some teachers get very concerned about distinguishing between content and process, for example, or between interest and learning profile. Don't let them get too worried about where something belongs in the grid because some items can overlap. The important thing is to encourage teachers to expand their repertoires of differentiation throughout a unit of study.

Incorporating Flexible Grouping into Unit Design (Advanced)

Activity

Refinement of good differentiated practices involves looking carefully at your use of differentiation over time. Sometimes we fall into a "differentiation rut" and forget that there are multiple ways to think about differentiating the content, processes, and products of a unit with regard to varied student readiness levels, interests, and learning profiles. This activity will help you identify gaps and expand your repertoire.

Directions:

1. Think about a particular unit of study. First, list all of the ways you have differentiated that unit in the past. Then, place each item on your list into an appropriate cell of the table below.
   - *Content* refers to the "stuff" kids have to learn, including the standards or benchmarks.
   - *Process* refers to the way students make sense of what they have to learn (e.g., activities).
   - *Product* refers to how students show us what they know, understand, and are able to do at the end of the unit.

Past Differentiation Efforts

	Content	Process	Product
Readiness			

Incorporating Flexible Grouping into Unit Design (Advanced)

Activity (Cont.)

	Content	Process	Product
Interest			
Learning Profile			

Incorporating Flexible Grouping into Unit Design (Advanced)

Activity (Cont.)

2. Study the idea grid below for suggestions of other ways to differentiate content, process, and products for readiness, interest, and learning profile. Note that, although we separate these elements for ease of learning, they may overlap considerably at times. (For example, if students are allowed to process via a preferred modality, they may be more ready for particular content.)

Idea Grid

	Content	Process	Product
Readiness	• Scaffold reading and find advanced texts. • Provide minilessons on above-grade-level content. • Provide minilessons on prerequisites. • Provide note-taking tools and/or vocabulary support (word banks).	• Allow students to dictate journal entries or other writing tasks (when appropriate). • Ask advanced students to work at a higher level of expertise or use more authentic materials or processes. (Remember, all students should work with authentic materials in ways similar to professionals in the field.) • Provide a set procedure for students to get extra help while working in the classroom. • Model the process and/or provide additional practice time for students who need it. • Provide practice opportunities (both in-class and as homework) at various levels of difficulty. • Break down the directions for students who need extra guidance.	• Require advanced students to work on products that are more expert-like or at a level of expertise appropriate to their growth. • Provide models of and rubrics for high-quality work. • Adjust time lines or check-in points for long-term projects. • Offer "polish-your-product" seminars for different levels of expertise. • Provide minilessons on aspects of the product. • Vary the audience for the product (e.g., some students might "present" their work to the local horticulture club while others "present" to a team of professors from the local agricultural university).

Part Three

Incorporating Flexible Grouping into Unit Design (Advanced)

Activity (Cont.)

	Content	Process	Product
Interest	• Have students become experts in one area of content and teach others (jigsaw method). • Design interest centers for the classroom. • Allow students to study content from a range of perspectives. • Assign independent research on a topic of choice (a composer, a New World explorer, a trigonometry application, etc.). • Assign novels with the same theme but different topics (adventure underwater, in the mountains, in space, etc.).	• Let students work with friends (when appropriate). • Provide mentoring opportunities. • Let students choose a lens through which they work (e.g., suggest they examine environmental issues as a chemist, a biologist, or a physicist might; allow them to show you that they understand the rules of perspective via a variety of artistic media; ask them to investigate a culture while acting as an anthropologist, a sociologist, an archaeologist, etc.).	• Allow students to show what they know through a lens of interest (e.g., show that they understand the effect of the jet stream on climate in a particular region of interest; show that they understand how sales tax works when buying their favorite toys).
Learning Profile	• Provide simultaneous options for accessing content that appeal to varied learning styles (e.g., lecture, small-group instruction, individual readings, reading buddies, books on tape, explorations). • Match topics to student intelligence preferences when possible (e.g., allow a musical student to focus on patriotic songs of a particular time and a student who is highly visual to study propaganda posters from the time). Jigsaw the content so all have access as appropriate. • Give the option to read text about the content before **or** after the lecture or direct instruction. • Provide the option to turn and chat or stop and think about the content as they listen or read.	• Allow students to work alone or in small groups (when appropriate). • Assign group roles according to learning profile preferences. • Provide a choice of graphic organizers (e.g., some that are more sequential in nature; others that are more random). • Give students the choice of competing against others or competing against themselves. • Allow students to keep pace while they read or listen (as long as it is not disruptive to others). • As much as possible, honor student requests about where to sit (e.g., up front, near the heater). • Allow students to debrief activities via journals or small-group discussions.	• Allow students to work alone or in small groups (when appropriate). • Allow for a wide range of product choices that represent varied styles, intelligence preferences, and cultural values. • Provide options for sharing products that respect student differences (e.g., allow students to present in front of the class, in a small group, or one-on-one).

Part Three

Incorporating Flexible Grouping into Unit Design (Advanced)

Activity (Cont.)

3. Return to your original grid. Look for gaps in your own practices. For example, do you tend to consider only reading readiness when you differentiate the content? Do you overrely on learning profile options for products? Now, complete a blank grid (or other organizer of your choice) for an upcoming unit of study. Try for a balance of differentiation of content, process, and product for readiness, interest, and learning profile throughout your unit.

Upcoming Unit Plan

	Content	Process	Product
Readiness			
Interest			
Learning Profile			

Tools for Teachers

Part Three

My Worries About Managing Differentiation

Rationale and Purpose

This tool helps teachers brainstorm about and begin to address management issues that often arise in the differentiated classroom. Use it to help you identify topics in this area that need further instruction.

Directions

- Distribute one copy of the graphic organizer to each teacher.
- Ask teachers to work alone to complete the organizer.
- Next, provide opportunities for them to share their worries with others and brainstorm possible solutions.
- Solicit ideas from the larger group for dealing with key worries.

Tips and Differentiation Options

- Collect the graphic organizers, and use the results to form study groups or plan follow-up staff development around managing the differentiated classroom.
- If you prefer, ask teachers to work in small groups to list their worries on chart paper. Then, have them brainstorm solutions. Have each group share its top worries and solutions, and ask the whole group to share any additional suggestions they have for these issues. Keep the lists for future staff development planning.

What to Look For

Typical questions that teachers ask:
- What if some students finish early or need more time?
- How will I explain why the activity is differentiated? Should I?
- What if one student needs help and I am busy with someone else?
- How do I give multiple sets of directions efficiently?
- What if students question which assignment I give them?
- What if I notice the assignment is not working for a child?
- How do I keep track of what everyone is doing?
- How do I decide who gets which version of each task? Should the students have a say?
- How do I distribute the differentiated assignments efficiently?

My Worries About Managing Differentiation

Activity

Directions:

- Use the boxes below to record your worries about managing a differentiated classroom.
- Compare your worries with those of your colleagues, and share possible solutions to the problems. You may want to note the name of the person(s) offering solutions in case you would like to get more information from them in the future.
- Which of these solutions can you implement immediately? Highlight those boxes.

My worry is . . .
A solution is . . .

My worry is . . .
A solution is . . .

My worry is . . .
A solution is . . .

My worry is . . .
A solution is . . .

My worry is . . .
A solution is . . .

My worry is . . .
A solution is . . .

Self-Assessment: Some Hot-Spot Areas in Leading the Multitask Classroom

ACTION TOOL

Rationale and Purpose

This tool provides an opportunity for teachers to identify areas of concern about managing the differentiated classroom.

Directions

- Distribute Part 1 of the assessment to each teacher. Ask them to rate their proficiency or comfort level with each of the listed "hot spots." Tell them they will not need to share this part of the assessment with you or with others.
- Distribute Part 2. Ask teachers to formulate goals for improving their comfort levels with managing the multitask classroom.

Tips and Differentiation Options

- You may collect Part 2 if you wish, or you may suggest that teachers incorporate one or more of these goals into their professional development portfolios.
- You may wish to have teachers complete Part 2 after you have provided general staff development in management issues. In other words, have teachers complete Part 1, provide an overview of strategies for dealing with common management concerns, then have teachers set goals. Information in the Keys to Successful Management of Differentiation tool (p. 213), may help you devise appropriate staff development modules.
- You can also use this assessment with administrators. Use the following directions:
  - Part 1: Analyze the specific needs of your school or a team of teachers in your school in terms of managing the multitask classroom. For each of the following management "hot spots" rate your teachers' proficiency on a scale from 1 (consistently a problem) to 5 (no problem whatsoever).
  - Part 2: Make a detailed plan for a staff development module that addresses an issue of particular concern to your staff. Be sure to consider how to introduce the issue, how to demonstrate possible approaches and solutions, how to honor current good practices while pushing teachers at all levels to refine their practices, and how to evaluate the effectiveness of your module on teacher practices.

ASCD
209

Self-Assessment: Some Hot-Spot Areas in Leading the Multitask Classroom

Activity

Part 1: For each of the following management "hot spots," rate your proficiency or comfort level on a scale from 1 (consistently a problem) to 4 (no problem whatsoever).

Issue	Rating
Explaining differentiation • to students. • to parents.	
Getting kids into groups quickly and efficiently.	
Giving directions when students are doing different things.	
Keeping kids on task when working • as a large group. • in small groups. • alone.	
Transitioning smoothly and efficiently from one activity to another.	

Self-Assessment: Some Hot-Spot Areas in Leading the Multitask Classroom

Activity (Cont.)

Issue	Rating
Teaching children how to work well in group settings.	
Handling "ragged time" (when kids finish at different times or work at different speeds).	
Keeping the noise level reasonable.	
Organizing for efficient access to materials and equipment.	
Delegating responsibility to students rather than doing it all yourself.	
Keeping track of who does what.	
Teaching kids to self-evaluate.	
Other (specify):	

Self-Assessment: Some Hot-Spot Areas in Leading the Multitask Classroom Activity (Cont.)

Part 2: Return to your hot-spot checklist, and choose three areas you would like to address or refine. Make a detailed plan for new ways to address each issue in your classroom. How and when will you evaluate your progress toward your goals?

Issue	How I Will Address the Issue	How and When I Will Evaluate My Progress

Keys to Successful Management of Differentiation

ACTION TOOL

Rationale and Purpose

When teachers work together, they become a rich source of practical ideas for solving classroom issues. This tool encourages teachers to work together to find solutions to common management issues.

Directions

- Write each of the questions in the left-hand column of the tool on a separate piece of chart paper.
- Seat teachers at tables of 4. Place one sheet on each table. Ask teachers to brainstorm ideas for handling the issue on their paper. They may appoint a scribe to record answers on the chart paper, or they may all write ideas on the paper at once.
- Have groups determine and then share their best responses to the issue.
- At the end of the activity, distribute copies of the Addressing Management Concerns chart. Point out the column where they may add their own ideas to the ideas provided.

Tips and Differentiation Options

- There is merit in seating teachers at tables homogeneously according to approximate grade level, so they can concentrate on what would work for specific age groups. There is equal merit in grouping them heterogeneously so that they are forced to come up with a range of ideas that may better match the needs of the whole group.
- You do not need to address all the questions at once. Choose a focus; for example, address only those questions dealing with having students work in groups.
- If you prefer, you can conduct this activity as a carousel:
  - Variation 1: Write each of the questions in the left-hand column of the tool on a separate piece of chart paper. Post the sheets of chart paper around the room. Divide up the teachers so that there are an even number of teachers at each sheet. (Two to three teachers per sheet works well.) Provide each teacher with a thin marker or pen. Give them 2 minutes to write as much as they can in response to the question. It is OK if they repeat someone else's answers. The focus is on brainstorming many answers. At the end of the allotted time, ring a bell and ask teachers to rotate clockwise to the next sheet. Remind them they should all write at once and that they can repeat answers. Repeat as many times as seems appropriate. Next, ask teachers to move to a question that particularly interests them. (Limit each question to 3–4 participants.) Provide 5–10 minutes for teachers to read the answers, categorize the responses, and come up with 1–3 "big ideas" expressing their best advice on how to handle that management issue. Ask one teacher at each station to report to the large group.

– Variation 2: If your space is limited or you are working with large numbers, choose five or six questions that you wish to focus on. Write each question in the middle of a separate sheet of chart paper. Seat teachers at tables of 4, and make enough sets of the questions so that you have one question per table. For example, if you have 40 teachers at 10 tables, make two sets of five questions. Determine a simple rotation pattern within each set of question sheets. Provide each teacher with a thin marker or pen. Tell them they will have 2 minutes to write as much as they can in response to the question and that it is OK if they repeat someone else's answers. The focus is on brainstorming many answers. At the end of the allotted time, ask one participant at each table to pass the sheet to the next table in the rotation. Remind them they should all write at once and that it is OK to repeat answers. Repeat until groups have their original sheet back again. Provide 5–10 minutes for teachers to read the answers, categorize the responses, and come up with 1–3 "big ideas" expressing their best advice on how to handle that management issue. Ask one teacher at each station to report to the large group.

What to Look For

- Teachers' understanding of each management concern and why it is important to address that concern in the differentiated classroom.
- Sound management practices that are feasible given realities of classroom space and student age.
- New ideas that teachers can add to their repertoire of management "tricks."

Keys to Successful Management of Differentiation

Addressing Management Concerns

Read the following thoughts about how to approach varied management concerns. Add your own ideas in the "My Ideas" column.

Worry	Thoughts	My Ideas
How do I decide who gets which version of each task?	Use all the information you have at your disposal to make the best decision you can. Sometimes you will want to decide who does which task or the exact composition of groups, and sometimes you will want to let the students decide. Teachers in a differentiated classroom base their decisions about who does what on a number of factors. The first three of these considerations are the most important:	
For group tasks, who should decide who works with whom?	• Your outcomes or KUD goals for the task and how keenly these goals depend upon an exact match between student needs and the task at hand—sometimes it is more important than other times that students get exactly the right match.	
	• Your confidence level in your knowledge of specific students' readiness, interests, and learning profiles—sometimes we have an excellent feel for what a student needs, and sometimes we are not so sure in spite of the evidence we have gathered.	
	• Your confidence level in your knowledge of group dynamics—sometimes we have an excellent feel for who should and should not work together and sometimes we are not so sure.	
	• Recent flexible grouping practices—variety is an important aspect of the differentiated classroom.	
	• The day of the week, mood of the students, timing of the task with respect to vacations, and so forth—students are more receptive to being told what to do or with whom they must work at certain times than others!	

Part Three

Keys to Successful Management of Differentiation

Addressing Management Concerns (Cont.)

Worry	Thoughts	My Ideas
How will I explain why the activity is differentiated? Should I?	Two principles are at work here: • It is vital that students and teachers in a differentiated classroom engage in ongoing, open, and honest dialogues about what differentiation is and why it occurs in their classroom. That differentiation occurs should never be a secret. Discuss the difference between "fair" and "equal," and create a class definition of "fair." • On the other hand, students don't need to have every instance of differentiation explicitly analyzed and thoroughly discussed. If we succeed in making differentiated activities equally engaging, challenging, and respectful, then students generally will not care—or even notice—that others are doing something different.	
Should the students have a say? If so, how?	Remember, it is important to allow students to make choices so that they know they have some control over their own learning. On the other hand, giving them too many choices may overwhelm them. Providing students with appropriate opportunities to make choices based on their interests can be a strong motivation for learning. Twin goals of the differentiated classroom are to get students to want to pick an appropriate level of challenge **and** to provide them with the tools with which to make that choice. This happens over time.	
What if the students question which assignment I give them or what I groups I place them in?	Remind students that sometimes they get to pick their assignments or who they work with, and other times you do. Sometimes students will balk at an assignment that they feel is too difficult. If you believe they are ready for the task, encourage them to take a risk and learn to enjoy a challenge. They may be uncomfortable at first, but let them know you have confidence in their readiness to do it. Provide the necessary scaffolding for students to achieve success on tasks that push them a little beyond their comfort zones.	

Keys to Successful Management of Differentiation

Addressing Management Concerns (Cont.)

Worry	Thoughts	My Ideas
What if I notice the task or group assignment is not working for a child?	Ask often for students' feedback about the match between task or group and their own needs. Make sure they know that they can tell you if an assignment is too easy or hard or doesn't quite fit in terms of interest or learning profile, and together you can try to find a solution. On the other hand, don't assume students will always come to you with this information. Be on the lookout for trouble spots, and make the necessary adjustments along the way. Talk openly with students about how and why you make the decisions you do, but make sure they know that you are always refining your techniques for matching student to task.	
What if I notice a group is not functioning well?	First of all, don't assume students know how to work in groups, no matter what grade level they are in. Teach them key group skills and what to do if they run into difficulty making their group function effectively. Remember that not all students like to work in groups, know the difference between effective and ineffective groups, or have the same level of interpersonal skill. You may need to differentiate the teaching of group skills, as well! For additional help with evaluating student readiness for group work, see Arter and McTighe's Group Interaction Rubric (2001, pp. 159–160) or the Teacher Checklist for Group Work in this book (p. 223).	

Part Three

Part Three

Keys to Successful Management of Differentiation

Addressing Management Concerns (Cont.)

Worry	Thoughts	My Ideas
How do I give multiple sets of directions efficiently?	It is generally not a good idea to give multiple sets of directions to the whole group. Besides wasting everyone's time, you will find that students will quickly lose interest in those directions that are not relevant to their task and may not notice when the directions *are* relevant! If a significant part of the instructions are the same for all students, then go ahead and present those to the large group. The rest of the instructions should be delivered to only those students who need them. Help students learn to listen to directions the first time you give them. We sometimes unwittingly teach students not to listen to instructions because they learn we will repeat ourselves numerous times. Routines such as designating an expert of the day to help with instructions or teaching students to "ask three before me" (students must ask three other students for help before they are allowed to ask you) are particularly useful. Such routines also free you to more quickly and efficiently handle unexpected issues that arise rather than answering the same questions over and over. Individual or group task cards are particularly effective ways to deliver instructions. You may find it useful to audio record the instructions so that students who do not read or who are auditory learners can play directions aloud. Check and recheck that your directions are clear so that you do not have numerous students asking you questions about what they should do. Many teachers find it useful to color-code instruction sheets or task cards so that they can quickly tell which set belongs to which activity.	

Keys to Successful Management of Differentiation

Addressing Management Concerns (Cont.)

Worry	Thoughts	My Ideas
How do I distribute the differentiated assignments and materials efficiently?	If you are sending students to different areas of the classroom to work, try to have the instructions and necessary materials already located in those areas. Plan ahead and try to anticipate any issues that might arise. Consider assigning jobs (e.g., materials handler, table captain) to different students when appropriate. A good general rule in any classroom is: "If the students can do it, let them!"	
How do I tell them which group they go to?	There are many routines for getting students into groups: • List groups, their members, and their assigned locations on the board. • Attach clothespins, magnets, or key tags with individual students' names on them to charts to delineate who does what and where to go. That way, you can group and regroup students as needed. • Place colored dots or sticky notes on students' desks before they enter to indicate the group they will join. • Place each version of a task on a separate sheet of colored paper. Distribute the sheets to the appropriate students, and then ask them to join others with the same color paper.	

Part Three

Part Three

Keys to Successful Management of Differentiation

Addressing Management Concerns (Cont.)

Worry	Thoughts	My Ideas
What if one student or group needs help and I am busy with someone else?	Teach students when it is OK to interrupt you and what to do when it is not. There are many routines that can help, such as teaching students to: • Ask for help from other students or the expert of the day. • Sign up on the board for a conference. • Use a table signal that they need help, such as displaying a red plastic cup or card when they are stuck, a yellow cup or card when they need help but can keep working on another part of their task, or a green cup or card when all is well. • Turn to an anchor activity until help is available. Remember the importance of practicing classroom routines and procedures. Simply stating the rules is not enough for most students.	
How will I get everyone's attention when necessary? **What if things get too noisy or chaotic?**	Set up routines for getting students' attention when necessary. Many teachers use a signal like playing a chime, flicking the lights, ringing a bell, or raising their hands while placing a finger to their mouths. Teach students what indoor voices do and don't sound like, how to move about the room quietly without bothering anyone, and other techniques for keeping order. Talk with the students about the importance of these routines, get them to help you brainstorm solutions, and determine consequences for students or groups who do not follow the rules.	

Keys to Successful Management of Differentiation

Addressing Management Concerns (Cont.)

Worry	Thoughts	My Ideas
What if some students or groups finish early or need more time?	Although this is an issue in any classroom, it is even more likely to occur in a differentiated classroom—especially early on, when you are getting used to designing differentiated activities that will take about the same amount of time. One approach to managing this situation is to design what is called an "anchor" activity: an ongoing assignment that students can work on independently throughout a unit, a grading period, or longer. The best anchor activities are meaningful work tied to unit or subject knowledge, understandings, and skills; have clear directions; can be done without disturbing others; and hold students accountable for quality and completion. **Anchor Activity Ideas** Better Than Nothing: • Brain teasers • Games, puzzles • Silent reading • Music listening stations • Other homework Better: • General interest learning packets • Learning or interest centers • Commercial kits and materials • Vocabulary work • Accelerated Reader program • Practice tests (unit, SAT, AP) Better Still: • Related course readings with questions or activities • Extension activities from text series • Journals or learning logs • Research or long-term class projects	

Part Three

Part Three

Keys to Successful Management of Differentiation

Addressing Management Concerns (Cont.)

Worry	Thoughts	My Ideas
How will I know students are really working in their groups?	Involve students in keeping track of their progress and evaluating their work, but remember to teach them how to do so. Provide a place for them to record not only what they did on a specific day but also how they think they did in terms of quality and quantity of work, as well as their work habits. For example:	
How do I keep track of what everyone is doing?	How Did I Do?	

How Did I Do?

What I did	:)	:|	:(
I worked hard.			
I did not bother anyone.			
I put away my materials.			

Next time, I will . . . .

What I planned to do	What I accomplished	What I need to work on next

Exit cards can be another quick way to check on student progress.

Plastic crates with hanging file folders for each student (use different colored crates for different class periods) can be a handy place for students to file their ongoing work. This gives you easy access to their work, too. Teach them what to do with their work once they complete it so that you are not inundated with papers at the end of class.

Keys to Successful Management of Differentiation

Teacher Checklist for Group Work

If you notice that a group is not functioning well, consult the following checklist, which identifies factors that contribute to effective group work (adapted from Tomlinson, 2005).

☐ Do students understand task goals? Are the directions perfectly clear?

☐ Does the task match the learning goals? Do students see a connection between what they are doing and what they need to learn?

☐ Do most kids find the task interesting? Feasible?

☐ Does the task require genuine collaboration to achieve genuine understanding?

☐ Does the task require an important contribution from each group member?

☐ Is the task demanding of members? Can all students contribute equally?

☐ Do students understand their own role in making the group work a success?

☐ Are the time lines brisk enough that students will want to get right to work?

☐ Are individuals and groups accountable for their own learning?

☐ Is there a way out for kids who are not succeeding? Do they know how and when to seek help?

☐ Are there opportunities for built-in teacher and peer coaching?

☐ Are there quality descriptors and checkpoints?

☐ Do students know what to do when "finished"?

Part Three

Keys to Successful Management of Differentiation

Activity

Directions:

- For this activity, you will work in table groups.
- Study the question on your chart paper. Brainstorm ideas for handling the issue, and write them anywhere on the paper. You may appoint a scribe to record answers, or you may all write ideas on the paper at once and then discuss them.
- Determine your best two or three suggestions for dealing with the issue, and be ready to share them with the large group.

Our Question:

Suggestion 1:
Suggestion 2:
Suggestion 3:

Tools for Teachers

Part Three

Is Differentiation Fair?

Rationale and Purpose

This tool helps teachers devise analogies about fairness to use with students and parents.

Directions

- Prepare four index cards, each with a different ailment listed on it:
  - Patient 1: You have a splitting headache.
  - Patient 2: You have a stomachache.
  - Patient 3: You have a broken arm.
  - Patient 4: You have a head trauma.
- Distribute one index card to each of four selected teachers. Tell them they will take part in a brief role-play. You will act as a doctor in a walk-in clinic, and the teachers will be patients who come for help. The ailment from which they are "suffering" is indicated on their index cards.
- Begin with Patient 1, and continue through Patient 4. Use the following script.

    Doctor: So, what is troubling you today?

    Patient: (Looks at card). I have a _____. What shall I do?

    Doctor: Hmmm . . . Take two aspirin, and call me in the morning.

- After the role-plays, ask teachers to talk about the ways in which this activity serves as an analogy for what happens in many classrooms.
- Present the following definition of fairness:

    Fairness is not necessarily giving every student the same thing; fairness is giving every student what they need to grow as much and as fast as they possibly can.

- Group teachers homogeneously according to grade level. Ask them to brainstorm and then share other analogies that they could use to help their students understand the fairness of differentiated instruction.

Tips and Differentiation Options

- If your group includes administrators, encourage them to focus on analogies that would help parents or the school board understand the fairness of differentiated instruction.
- Alternate activity: Provide the following options for teachers as a follow-up to the doctor/patient demonstration:
  - Practical Thinkers: Describe how you handle the fairness issue when it arises in your own classroom.
  - Creative Thinkers: What analogy can you think of that would help your students understand the differentiation definition of fairness?
  - Analytical Thinkers: How fair is the one-size-fits-all classroom?

What to Look For

- Analogies that are clear and age-appropriate.
- Accurate interpretation of differentiation and its role in the heterogeneous classroom.

Is Differentiation Fair?

Activity

You have just seen an example of how an analogy can make an important point about a totally unrelated situation. In this case, we compared a doctor's response to patients with varied ailments to a teacher's response to students with different instructional needs.

What other analogies can you think of that would help your students (or their parents) understand why differentiation is fair? Summarize your ideas below.

Part Three

What About Standards?

Rationale and Purpose

This tool helps teachers confront their own and others' questions about the compatibility of the standards movement with differentiated instruction.

Directions

- Place each provided bulleted thought on a separate slip of paper.
- Distribute one slip to each teacher; tell them not to read the slips until you give a signal.
- Display the discussion questions from the tool on the board or overhead projector, or give each teacher a copy of the activity sheet provided. Give teachers some time to jot down their thoughts in response to the questions.
- Ask teachers to partner with someone at a different table. Ask them to share the thoughts on their slips of paper and their immediate reactions to them. Then, they should use the discussion questions to explore the extent to which the thoughts might help them (as well as students and parents) wrestle with the seeming disconnect between the push for common standards for all students and the need for differentiated instruction to meet those standards.
- Ask teachers to change partners and repeat the process as many times as practical.
- Finally, ask teachers to compose a brief answer in their own words to one of the reflection questions provided.

Tips and Differentiation Options

- If you prefer, ask teachers to form two concentric circles; the inside circle facing out and the outside circle facing in. Have them share their thoughts as above, and then ask the inside circle to rotate clockwise and the outside circle to rotate counterclockwise so that they have a new partner. Repeat as appropriate.
- If you prefer to work as a whole group, display selected quotes and ask teachers to think, pair, and share their reactions. Ask teachers to write out their answers to the final questions on an exit card. Collect and review their answers to see what issues you still need to address.
- You may wish to collect the responses to reflection questions to help you consider teachers' needs in terms of dealing with this issue.

What to Look For

- Teachers who are having a hard time distinguishing between **what** we teach and **how** we teach will need further support with a rationale for differentiation.

- To some teachers, standards-based teaching is all about telling students what they need to know. They are afraid that in standards-based classrooms, there is little or no time for inquiry-based or hands-on instruction. If this is the case with some of your staff, you will need to correct this misconception.

- If teachers feel that they are required to use scripted instructional materials or keep exact pace with their colleagues at all times, it will be difficult for them to embrace differentiation.

- Help teachers see that although helping students meet standards is exceedingly important—and a part of every teacher's job description—student growth over time is also valuable. In other words, if a student starts out the year at the 30th percentile and moves to the 55th percentile by the end of the year, he or she will still be "below standard." Nevertheless, there would be much for both the teacher and the student to celebrate.

What About Standards?

Thoughts About Differentiation

- Standards are **what** we teach. Differentiation is **how** we teach. —Carol Ann Tomlinson

- A textbook and a set of standards do not a curriculum make. Rather they are some ingredients for a meal, not a meal in and of itself. —Carol Ann Tomlinson

- A standard by itself is impotent. . . . It needs to be activated by the teacher to allow students access to powerful concepts and principles. —Sandra Kaplan

- The goal of standards-based curriculum is to provide an equitable and excellent education for all learners —the reality is that there is no such thing as a standard that is appropriately challenging for all learners. —Carol Ann Tomlinson

- For highly able learners who may already demonstrate mastery of standards or who master them in less time than others, standards-based instruction may result in a curriculum of waiting rather than growth. —Carol Ann Tomlinson

- Educators need to stick to standards but should also consider how they might vary their teaching of those standards to ensure instruction is a good fit for a wide range of learners. —Holly Gould (2000)

- We might temporarily simplify the requirements for some students, but that does not mean we will eliminate the benchmarks. We'll reinsert those goals as soon as it's developmentally appropriate to do so. —Rick Wormeli (2007, p. 21)

- Students who are the same age differ in their readiness to learn, their interests, their styles of learning, their experiences, and their life circumstances. The differences in students are significant enough to make a major impact on what students need to learn, the pace at which they need to learn it, and the support they need from teachers and others to learn it well. —Carol Ann Tomlinson (2000)

- Standards-based education and differentiation not only can coexist, but must function together as two sides of the same accountability coin —Jay McTighe & John Brown (2005, p. 235)

- While standards may direct your curriculum and focus your learning goals, they *don't* dictate what you do instructionally to get students "there." —Diane Heacox (2002, p. 14)

- It would be ludicrous to practice for the doctor's physical exam as a way of becoming fit and well. The reality is the opposite: If we are physically fit and do healthy things, we will pass the physical. The separate items on the physical are not meant to be taught and crammed for: rather they serve as indirect measures of our normal healthful living. —Jay McTighe & Grant Wiggins (2001, p. 132)

What About Standards?

Thoughts About Differentiation (Cont.)

- Standards do not imply one-size-fits-all standardization of professional practice. —Jay McTighe & John Brown (2005, p. 243)

- When we differentiate, we give students the tools to handle whatever comes their way—differentiated or not. This is why differentiated instruction and standardized testing are not oxymoronic: Students will do well on standardized, undifferentiated tests only if they have learned the material in the class, and differentiated practices are the ways we maximize students' learning at every turn. —Rick Wormeli (2006, p. 4)

Part Three

What About Standards?

Activity

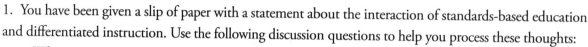

1. You have been given a slip of paper with a statement about the interaction of standards-based education and differentiated instruction. Use the following discussion questions to help you process these thoughts:

    •   What is your immediate reaction to each thought or idea?

    •   Do you disagree or agree with the speakers? Why?

    •   Are these ideas new or familiar?

    •   To what extent does each match or not match your own understanding of standards-based instruction? Your own philosophy of teaching?

    •   To what extent do the thoughts help you, your students, and their parents wrestle with the seeming disconnect between the push for common standards for all students and the need for differentiated instruction to meet those standards?

What About Standards?

Activity (Cont.)

2. When the leader gives the signal, pair up with a partner and share your thoughts.

3. Repeat the process with a new partner.

4. Work alone to prepare a brief written or oral response to one of the questions below.

Reflection Questions (choose one):

____ How can teachers be expected to differentiate when they are told that everyone must meet the same standards?

____ To what extent is the standards movement compatible with differentiated instruction?

____ How do you justify differentiating in a standards-based environment?

My Response:

What About Standardized Tests?

Rationale and Purpose

This tool helps teachers tackle the worry that students in a differentiated classroom will end up unprepared for standardized, undifferentiated testing experiences.

Directions

- Pair teachers at random, or ask them to choose partners. Tell them they will engage in a forced-choice debate. One of them will take the position that "Students in a differentiated classroom are at a **disadvantage** when it comes to taking a standardized, one-size-fits-all test." The other will take the position that "Students in a differentiated classroom are at an **advantage** when it comes to taking a standardized, one-size-fits-all test." Tell them there is to be no compromising; they must steadfastly represent their side of the issue. Give teachers about 3–5 minutes to debate the issue.

- Ask for one volunteer from each side to conduct a debate in front of the whole group.

- Debrief the experience. Ask: "How can we justify differentiating instruction when all students have to take the same test on the same day?"

- Finally, ask teachers to compose a brief answer in their own words to one of the reflection questions provided.

Tips and Differentiation Options

- To pair teachers, have them choose from a bag of mixed hard candies as they enter the room. Tell them not to eat the candy yet. When you give the signal, they should pair up with someone who has the kind of candy they have.

- Another way to pair teachers: As teachers enter the room, hand them a blue or a green paper clip. Tell them to pair up with someone whose paper clip is the other color. Assign the side of the debate according to color. For example, if teachers have a blue clip, they are on the **advantage** side; if they have a green clip, they are on the **disadvantage** side.

- In the whole-group sharing, instead of asking a pair of teachers to debate, you can take the side that students in a differentiated classroom are at a disadvantage and ask the teachers to work as a whole to take the advantage side. Start off by saying something like: "You, know, now that I think about it, it would be a real disservice to students if we differentiate in the classroom, knowing that the state test (or AP test) is not differentiated." Ask for volunteers to react to your statement. Work hard to shoot down any counterarguments they raise, but eventually "give in."

- You may wish to collect the responses to reflection questions to help you consider teachers' needs in terms of dealing with this issue.

What to Look For

- If teachers are differentiating well, students should have significant advantages when it comes time to take a standardized test. Make sure the comments against differentiating do not represent misconceptions about differentiation. For example, students do **not** always get to work in preferred ways in a differentiated classroom. They should have a balance of opportunities to work in preferred and less-preferred modalities. Furthermore, when the goal of an activity is writing, teachers in a high-quality differentiated classroom do not give the choice of writing an essay, preparing a PowerPoint, or making a speech. Everyone writes an essay, although some students may get more support than others as they write.

- Students who experience success in the classroom will have a more positive outlook going into the test. This should help them perform better overall. It does little good to teach students content that they are not ready for. It is better to teach them at an appropriate level and work to accelerate the speed of their progress to get as close to grade-level standards as possible in the time provided. Even if these students do not "pass" the test, they should get a significantly better score than they would have without appropriate instruction. We need to celebrate progress toward standards as well as attainment of standards.

- Advanced students will likely pass the test, anyway, but a differentiated classroom will help them continue to grow, teaching them valuable work habits that they will need later in life. Too many advanced students do not experience the satisfaction of hard work leading to success at school. When they are finally challenged, they may not know how to approach the situation.

What About Standardized Tests?

Activity

Directions:

1. You will be paired with another teacher for this forced-choice debate activity. One of you will take the position that students in a differentiated classroom are at a **disadvantage** when it comes to taking a standardized, one-size-fits-all test. The other will take the position that students in a differentiated classroom are at an **advantage** when it comes to taking a standardized, one-size-fits-all test. Steadfastly represent your assigned side of the issue. You will have 5 minutes to conduct your debate.

2. The facilitator will help you debrief the experience. Your goal is to be able to answer the following question: "How can we justify differentiating instruction when all students have to take the same test on the same day?"

Reflection Questions (choose one):

____ How can teachers be expected to differentiate when they are told that everyone must meet the same standards?

____ To what extent is the standards movement compatible with differentiated instruction?

____ How do you justify differentiating in a standards-based environment?

My Response:

Introduction to Grading in the Differentiated Classroom (Entry Points)

Rationale and Purpose

Entry points, as described by Howard Gardner (1991), provide multiple doorways through which students may "enter into" a unit of study. Entry points respond primarily to learning profile and interest, although they may also be tiered for readiness. Because entry points activities serve as a short hook for a unit of study, each activity must not necessarily lead to the same KUD goals. In this case, the tool uses entry points as a way to both activate teachers' prior knowledge and raise their awareness of concerns about common grading practices. This tool also serves as a model of this differentiated strategy, with the hope that teachers will find a way to incorporate it into their own classrooms.

Directions

- Distribute the tool. Ask teachers to read through the activities and choose the one that most interests them.
- Specify a part of the room for each activity, and have participants report there to work with others with the same interest. Allow teachers about 15 minutes to complete their task.
- Reconvene as a whole group, and ask teachers to share key insights or concerns about grading in general and in the differentiated classroom.
- Ask teachers to answer the reflection questions about the entry points strategies and share their thoughts in small groups or in the whole-group setting.

Tips and Differentiation Options

- It is not necessary that all entry points be covered. However, you may wish to limit the number of participants at a particular station. In that case, ask teachers to have an alternate entry point in mind if their first choice is full.
- If you prefer, after teachers have discussed grading in entry points groups, regroup them so that there are a variety of entry points represented at each table. Ask them to share any insights they now have into issues surrounding grading.
- Grading discussions can get quite heated because they often reflect very personal—and valid—experiences with grades. There is no one "right way" to grade. Remind teachers that this (and future) discussions about grading are an opportunity to look at our practices in new ways. We need to be respectful of differing philosophies and beliefs. At the same time, we need to be open to a thoughtful examination of past and current practices.

What to Look For

- As you circulate, listen for clues to teachers' differing philosophies about grading. Listen, too, for misconceptions and myths.

- Keep an eye out for teachers who are particularly distressed by this topic, and speak to them individually about their concerns.

Introduction to Grading in the Differentiated Classroom

Entry Points Activities

We are beginning an exploration of the issues surrounding grading and assessment in the differentiated classroom. Choose one of the following entry points activities, and report to that station. Complete the activity as directed. Once you have finished, respond to the reflection questions provided.

Entry Point	Description	Your Task
Narrational	Read or tell a story or narrative	Do you have a grading story to tell? Share a time when you or someone you know was unfairly affected by grading. What went wrong? How might the situation have been improved?
Logical-Quantitative	Provide data; use deductive reasoning; examine numbers, statistics, musical rhythm, logic, narrative plot structure, cause-and-effect relationships	What confounds grades? Choose one of the following practices, and show mathematically how it can affect students for the better and/or for the worse: • Averaging grades • Use of zeros • Extra-credit assignments • Grading **everything** a student does
Foundational	Confront big questions of philosophy and meaning concerning life, death, and our place in the world	Choose from the following discussion questions: • Why grade? • What is a grade? • What does a grade represent? What should it represent? • How do grades affect life after high school? • What makes for a "fair" grade?
Aesthetic	Study sensory and/or surface features, activate aesthetic sensitivities	Assign the role of a student with a particular "label" (special education, learning disabled, gifted, English language learner, etc.) to each group member. Put yourself in the shoes of that student. In character, discuss your feelings about grades.

Introduction to Grading in the Differentiated Classroom

Entry Points Activities (Cont.)

Entry Point	Description	Your Task
Experiential (also known as experimental)	Deal directly with materials (physically or virtually), simulations, personal explanations; a hands-on approach	Imagine the following scenarios. Share your reactions to each one. 1. Health and Wellness has been given a grant of $1,000 to encourage teachers to lose weight. At the end of 9 weeks, the money goes to the teacher who has lost the most weight. 2. Health and Wellness has been given a grant of $1,000 to encourage teachers to lose weight. At the end of nine weeks, the money goes to one teacher, based on a combination of the following factors: • Amount of weight lost • Percentage of starting weight lost • Attitude and effort put into weight loss Extra points are given to teachers who do an extra-credit project on the relationship between weight loss and diet and exercise. 3. Health and Wellness has been given three grants of $350 each to encourage teachers to lose weight. • One grant will go to the teacher who loses the most weight. • One grant will go to the teacher whose percentage loss is greatest. • One grant will go to the teacher who shows up to all the weigh-ins on time; keeps careful—and neat—track of all eating and exercise; tries his or her best to lose weight; and maintains a good attitude throughout the process.

Introduction to Grading in the Differentiated Classroom

Activity Reflection

In what way(s) was this activity differentiated?

How did you decide which activity to complete? Did you make a good choice? Explain.

What were the common learning goals in this activity?

What other ways might we differentiate an introduction to grading?

How might you incorporate an entry points activity into your own curriculum?

Part Three

Perspectives on Grading (RAFT)

Rationale and Purpose

This tool works well as an introduction or a culmination to a discussion on grading issues. It also provides a model of the differentiated RAFT strategy.

Directions

- Distribute or display the RAFT. Explain that RAFT is a strategy that assigns a role, identifies an audience, suggests a format to work in, and provides a topic to address. The different rows in a RAFT may be designed to respond to differences in student interest, learning profile, and/or readiness.
- Ask teachers to pair up with a colleague and choose the horizontal row they wish to complete. Suggest they choose a role with which they can identify (interest) or a format that is comfortable for them (learning profile).
- If teachers have other ideas for RAFT rows, ask them to check with you for approval.
- When everyone is finished or at the end of a set period of time, ask teachers to share their work with the large group or in small mixed-role groups.
- Solicit ideas for how and when teachers might use the RAFT strategy in their own classrooms.
- Ask teachers to complete an exit card that gives an example of what one row of a RAFT might look like in their own subject area.

Tips and Differentiation Options

- Allow teachers to work alone if they prefer.
- If you wish to ensure a variety of roles, limit how many pairs may complete each row.
- Remind teachers that if they use this strategy with students, they should be sure that students know the properties of the various formats (poster, speech, poem, etc.).

What to Look For

- If using this as an introductory activity, watch for indications of teachers' beliefs about the role and impact of grading in today's schools.
- If using this as a culminating activity, watch for changes in beliefs about grading, as well as concerns that still need to be addressed.
- Note the quality of each product. Although the information communicated is clearly more important than the actual product, product quality also matters. Point out particularly good examples of a specific product—for example, a flowchart that is easy to follow and takes into account alternate routes.
- Consider sharing some or all of the examples from the exit cards at a later session.

Perspectives on Grading

RAFT Activity

Work alone or with a partner. Choose one of the following rows, and complete the assignment together. If you have a different idea, consult the facilitator and fill it in at the bottom of the chart.

ROLE	AUDIENCE	FORMAT	TOPIC
Teacher	Students	Poem or parable	Definition of "fair"
Teacher	Parents	Short speech at Parent Night	Why I grade students
College supervisor	Student teacher	Top 10 list	What you really need to know about grading
Heterogeneous class	Teacher	Rule book	How we would handle grading if we were teachers
A student who finds school difficult and stressful	Parent-teacher organization	Show-and-tell presentation	What I like best about grades
A student from a low-income home	Other students	Comic strip	Why I dislike most grades
Student just learning English	Students fluent in English	Flowchart	What "fair" should mean in the classroom
A highly able student	AP teacher	Conference presentation	What it means to say a teacher really challenges me
Teacher	Self	Pep talk to self	Things about grading I control

Part Three

Perspectives on Grading

RAFT Activity (Cont.)

ROLE	AUDIENCE	FORMAT	TOPIC
Teacher	Colleagues	Argument presented at a faculty meeting	Why we should outlaw grades
Struggling student	Principal	An illustration with labels	How effort does or doesn't pay off for me in school
My Idea:			

Source: Adapted with permission from the work of Carol Ann Tomlinson, Curry School of Education, University of Virginia.

Practically Speaking: Grading in the Differentiated Classroom

Rationale and Purpose

Some teachers cannot even begin to consider differentiated practices without thinking about how they might grade them. This tool provides practical advice for dealing with teacher worries about grading. The suggestions offered are not perfect, but they may help reluctant teachers reluctant get started.

Directions

- Discuss the possible impact of differentiated practices on grading and reporting practices. Ask: Is it harder or easier to grade well in the differentiated classroom than in a more "traditional" classroom?
- Tell teachers that the complex issues surrounding grading practices are unlikely to be solved quickly. For practical advice on how to deal with grading in the meantime, direct them to the suggestions on the tool. Ask them to jot down the pros and cons of each suggestion and then discuss each suggestion's merits as a group. Ask them to share other ideas for approaching grading in the differentiated classroom.

Tips and Differentiation Options

- If you conduct the discussion in small groups, group teachers homogeneously by grade level (primary, upper elementary, middle, high) or heterogeneously by subject area.
- Teachers tend to be hungry for a definitive answer on how to grade differentiated assignments. Some become quite frustrated at the ambiguities involved. Be sensitive to their concerns.
- It may help teachers to come to a consensus as a grade level or subject team about how to handle grading differentiated assignments. Sometimes there is safety in numbers!
- Consider appointing a subcommittee of interested teachers to explore best practices in grading and report back to the larger group. Suggest that they use the Helpful Resources on Grading to start their research.

Part Three

Practically Speaking: Grading in the Differentiated Classroom

Grading Suggestions

If you are worried about grading in the differentiated classroom:

- Start introducing kids to the idea of the three pillars of grading (below). Help them see the importance of mastery of subject; continual growth no matter where they begin their journey towards mastery; and practicing and refining work habits (participating, completing work on time, cooperating with others, etc.) throughout that journey. Best-practices grading would report information about the pillars *separately*. Note the three pillars are not meant to be averaged together. That defeats the purpose. Even though you may have to keep your current "official" grading system for now, you can at least start reporting information about mastery, growth, and work habits independently to students throughout, and particularly at the end of, a grading period.

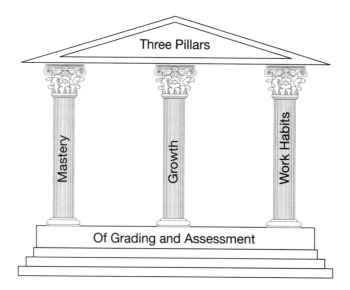

- Continually and consistently talk about fairness and how it affects grading: Is it fair for some people to get *A*s without working? Is it fair for some kids to never get *A*s, even though they work hard and learn a lot?
- Differentiate activities that are not graded or are graded only for completion; if students do the assignment to your satisfaction, give them full credit, but if not, have them redo it.
- Begin your differentiation efforts around differences in student learning profile and interest; students seem to feel there is a lot less at stake when they get to choose according to those aspects of differentiation. Work up to differentiation by readiness.
- When differentiating for readiness, let advanced kids choose whether to do the "harder" (more appropriate) assignment, but push them individually to choose what is actually the right match for them.

Practically Speaking: Grading in the Differentiated Classroom

Grading Suggestions (Cont.)

- When differentiating for readiness, ask advanced kids to do the appropriate assignment and give them serious feedback about how they did on the task, but give them an *A* for the project if you feel that's what they would have gotten on the grade-level assignment. Be careful, though! The problem with this "solution" is its implication for students who struggle—does this mean they can only get a *B* or *C* on an assignment because they are working below grade level? What if they do their absolute best on an assignment that is appropriately challenging? Should they not get an *A* on that assignment? (Note that this would not really be an issue if we moved to the idea of three-pillar grading.)
- No matter how you differentiate an assignment (for interest, learning profile, or readiness), always evaluate the KUD goals first and the product second; that way, all students are responsible for the same knowledge, understandings, and skills even if the products vary or are at varied levels of difficulty. Use the following questions to help you write rubric descriptors for the KUD goals:

KNOW	Do students include important facts, vocabulary, definitions, and people in their work?
	To what extent do students show a mastery of these facts, vocabulary, definitions, and people?
	To what degree is their use of facts, vocabulary, definitions, and people accurate and appropriate?
	How deep is their knowledge?
	How broad is their knowledge?
UNDERSTAND	Is there evidence that students have an understanding of the "big ideas" or key principles of the unit?
	To what degree do they appropriately and correctly incorporate these ideas into their work?
	How sophisticated, creative, and detailed is their understanding of unit principles?
	Have they identified additional principles that might apply?
BE ABLE TO DO	Can students identify and perform the skills embedded in the unit?
	Do they or can they use these skills in isolation and in combination?
	To what extent and at what level of expertise do they use the skills?
	Do they show evidence of more advanced skills key to the task but not focused on in the current unit of study?

Practically Speaking: Grading in the Differentiated Classroom

Helpful Resources on Grading

Brookhart, S. M. (2003). *Grading*. Upper Saddle River, NJ: Prentice-Hall.

Guskey, T. R. (2002). *How's my kid doing? A parent's guide to grades, marks, and report cards*. San Francisco: Jossey-Bass.

Guskey. T. R., & Bailey, J. M. (2001). *Developing grading and reporting systems for student learning*. Thousand Oaks, CA: Corwin.

Marzano, R. J. (2000). *Transforming classroom grading*. Alexandria, VA: Association for Supervision and Curriculum Development.

O'Connor, K. (2002). *How to grade for learning* (2nd ed.). Thousand Oaks, CA: Corwin.

O'Connor, K. (2007) *A repair kit for grading: 15 fixes for broken grades*. Princeton. NJ: ETS.

Whitney, D. T., Culligan, J. J., & Brooksher, P. T. (2004). *Truth in grading: Troubling issues with learning assessment*. Lincoln, NE: iUniverse.

Wormeli, R. (2006). *Fair isn't always equal: Assessing and grading in the differentiated classroom*. Portland, ME: Stenhouse.

Practically Speaking: Grading in the Differentiated Classroom

Activity

Review the grading suggestions that you were given, and record your thoughts about the pros and cons of each in the chart below.

Suggestion	Pros	Cons

Communicating with Parents About Differentiation

Rationale and Purpose

Helping parents understand the philosophy and practices of the differentiated classroom is a key factor in being successful with this model. This tool will help teachers plan answers to questions that parents are likely to ask about differentiation.

Directions

- Begin by asking teachers to generate a list of questions they think that parents will have about differentiation.
- Distribute the tool. Ask teachers to add any additional questions that were raised during the discussion. Point out that each question on the tool has a series of "talking points" to help participants formulate a response.
- Divide up the questions among groups of teachers. Ask them to formulate response to the questions that would be suitable for use in a school newsletter or at a back-to-school night, for example.
- Share responses with the large group as appropriate.

Tips and Differentiation Options

- Small groups of 2–4 that are homogeneous in terms of grade level (primary, upper elementary, middle, high) and heterogeneous in terms of teacher experience work best for this activity.
- If teachers prefer to work alone, let them do so.
- Collect the responses, and use them to formulate school- or districtwide information pamphlets about differentiated instruction as appropriate.
- Vary the product. For example, some teachers might work on a brochure to distribute to prospective parents visiting the district. Others might write a formal letter to parents or an article for the school newspaper. Still others might work on a speech or a PowerPoint presentation for a back-to-school night.

What to Look For

Teachers should use the talking points in the tool to form appropriate responses.

Communicating with Parents About Differentiation

Activity

Use the following talking points to help you formulate possible responses to parental concerns about differentiated instruction. Add your own questions and responses to the rows at the bottom.

Question	Talking Points	My Response
Is differentiation fair?	• Realities of the diversity in today's classrooms • New definition of fair • Equity of opportunity and access to high-quality teaching and instruction • Definition of appropriate challenge	
How will I know how my child is doing?	• Available avenues of communication • Separate reporting for grade-level standing, growth over time, and work habits	
How will you grade differentiated assignments?	• Focus on KUD goals • Three pillars of grading • Your own philosophy of grading	
How will you know what my child needs? How will you make sure that you challenge my child appropriately? How will you avoid typecasting my child?	• Pre-assessment • Ongoing assessment • Teacher–student partnerships in matching student to task	
Won't students feel like you have labeled them?	• Definition and practice of flexible grouping • Helping students make an honest assessment of their strengths and weaknesses • Respect for potential of all students regardless of "label"	

Part Three

Communicating with Parents About Differentiation

Activity (Cont.)

Part Three

Question	Talking Points	My Response
Why do you teach this way? That's not how school was for us.	• Changes in schools and society • Right of all students to grow • Right of all students to high-quality teaching and learning	
Life's not differentiated, so why should schools be differentiated?	• Life is more differentiated than we like to think. • Everyone needs to get along with and appreciate others. • The differentiated classroom celebrates similarities **and** differences among learners.	

Tools for Teachers

Differentiation Bingo (Anchor Activity)

Rationale and Purpose

This tool provides not only a model of an anchor activity but also a structure for teachers' experimentation with differentiation elements and strategies.

Directions

- Distribute the bingo card.
- Explain that anchor activities are purposeful work related to unit or subject goals that students are taught to turn to if they finish early or are waiting for help from the teacher. Anchor activities should generally be independent work.
- Tell teachers how long they will have to complete their first bingo. Remind them that they should attach evidence of their work to the bingo card.
- Ask teachers:
  - What do you normally ask students to do if they finish something early?
  - How might you use a bingo card or other anchor strategy in your own classroom?
  - Why is it so important that anchor activities respond to student interest, learning profile, and/or readiness?
  - Should anchor activities be graded? Why or why not?

Tips and Differentiation Options

- Change the bingo options according to elements and strategies that your teachers have already been exposed to. This is not the place for new content.
- At a prior session, ask teachers to brainstorm small steps that they could take to improve their comfort and familiarity with classroom practices that support differentiation. Use their suggestions as bingo squares.
- Depending on your time frame and teachers' familiarity with differentiation, you may wish to make this a tic-tac-toe rather than a bingo.
- If you prefer, ask teachers to complete a certain number of squares over the course of a semester or year rather than forcing them to make a bingo. If they do get a bingo, however, it often ensures they balance their work in areas that are both comfortable and less comfortable for them (a key tenet of differentiation).
- If you have time, ask teachers to make a bingo-like card (or other anchor activity) for use in their own classroom.

Part Three

What to Look For

- Evidence that teachers fulfilled the spirit of the tasks and that they reflected on the impact of the activity.
- Squares that no one chose. This may indicate a need for further instruction or discussion about that strategy.

Differentiation Bingo

Bingo Card

Try to make one bingo between now and the end of the year. Attach evidence of your work and a brief reaction to each experience, and submit it to your staff development leader.

B	I	N	G	O
Provide students with a choice of graphic organizer.	Give students a choice of activities or products that are differentiated for learning profile. Ask them to work in their preferred style or modality.	Read an article or chapter on differentiation. Write a brief reaction to the reading.	Talk to students or parents about why you differentiate **or** the meaning of "fair."	Provide advanced students with an advanced text or reading assignment.
Teach a minilesson to review or reinforce knowledge, understanding, or skill.	Design and carry out an activity in which students work in a group with others who are unlike them in interests, learning profile, or readiness.	Offer product options for a culminating assessment.	Give students the choice of working alone or with another person.	Ask students to choose an activity or product option that is **not** in their preferred learning modality. Have them reflect on that experience.
Ask students to self-evaluate their work according to set criteria.	Observe another teacher differentiating, **or** provide that teacher with feedback on a differentiated task.	FREE: Your choice of activity that supports differentiation.	Teach a minilesson to extend knowledge, understanding, or skill.	Change grouping of students at least once during a class period. Be sure your groupings are purposeful, not random.
Share a differentiated activity at a school or department staff meeting.	Differentiate a homework assignment for interest, learning profile, or readiness.	Design and carry out an activity in which students work in a group with others who are like them in interests, learning profile, or readiness.	Assign classroom or group jobs.	Help students learn about the difference between a functional group and a dysfunctional group.
Design and introduce an anchor activity that is clearly tied to your unit or course goals.	Design and use an exit card for ongoing assessment.	Scaffold your text or a reading assignment to support students who struggle with reading.	Pre-assess for interest, learning profile, or readiness.	Provide audio support for a text or reading assignment.

Part Three

Differentiated Strategies Menu

ACTION TOOL

Rationale and Purpose

This tool provides another format for organizing teacher work in differentiation over the course of a semester or school year. It also models the contract strategy.

Directions

- Share information about how contracts fit the differentiation model.
    - Contracts are essentially an agreement between student and teacher. The teacher grants certain freedoms and choices about what students will work on; how, when, and where they will work; and the order in which they will complete tasks. The student agrees to use the freedoms appropriately.
    - Contracts often have certain tasks that all students must do along with a certain number of choice activities. Sometimes they also include optional activities.
    - Contracts most often offer choices in response to varied interests and learning profiles but can also be tiered for student readiness. In designing a contract, be sure that students are able to meet the KUD goals no matter which choices they make. Enrichment activities make great optional activities for contracts.
- Ask teachers to share their own experiences with contracts.
- Distribute a copy of the menu to each teacher.
- Tell them when the contract is due.
- Point out that they may substitute a dessert for two side dishes (because the desserts are more complex and involve a certain amount of intellectual and social risk).
- Remind them to attach evidence of their work to their contract.

Tips and Differentiation Options

- Adjust the tasks to match the focus of your work so far on differentiation.
- Consider offering a different set of tasks for teachers at varied levels of readiness with differentiation or with teaching in general.

What to Look For

- Evidence that teachers accurately and appropriately implemented the strategies in the contract.
- Options no one chose. This may indicate a need for further instruction in or discussion about those strategies.

Differentiated Strategies Menu

Menu Activity

Part Three

Menu: DIFFERENTIATION OF INSTRUCTION

Due Date:

You must complete all items in the main dish and the specified number of side dishes by the due date. You may select the indicated number of choices from among the side dishes, and you may decide to do some of the dessert items, as well. Please highlight the options you choose. Initial and date each item when completed. Attach evidence of your work to this contract, and turn it in to the facilitator.

Main Dish (Complete all.)

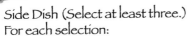

- Design a tiered activity with 2–4 levels. Be sure you include clear KUD goals for the activity.
- Carry out the activity in your classroom.
- Write a one- or two-paragraph summary of how it went and what you would do differently next time.

Side Dish (Select at least three.)
For each selection:

- Choose from the following activities to carry out in your classroom.
- Jot down notes on how they went and what you would do differently next time.

Options:
- Activity based on Sternberg's intelligences (creative, practical, and analytical)
- Learning contract
- Entry points activity
- Pre-assessment for readiness
- Pre-assessment for interest or learning profile
- RAFT assignment
- Cubing or ThinkDots activity
- Differentiated learning center
- Compacting for a student or group
- Another differentiated strategy you have read about
- Anchor activity that extends or reinforces a unit of study

Dessert (Optional or may take the place of two side dishes)
- Present your differentiated activity to the staff; include visuals. Be ready to say what worked well and what you would change next time.
- Watch a colleague teach a differentiated lesson, and meet to provide feedback.
- Teach a differentiated lesson while being observed by a colleague. Meet afterward to get feedback.
- Invite your principal to observe you teach a differentiated lesson. Meet to get feedback.
- E-mail a differentiated activity to a colleague, instructional coach, or administrator for feedback before you teach the lesson and send a reflection for feedback after you teach the lesson.

Summarizing the Components of Differentiation (Sternberg Intelligence Preferences)

Rationale and Purpose

This tool can be used to help teachers synthesize their learning about an aspect of differentiated instruction (interest) and, at the same time, model a Sternberg intelligence activity (learning profile).

Directions

- Ask teachers to choose and complete the activity that will provide them with the best opportunity to show what they know, understand, and can do with differentiation.
- As a follow-up, ask for volunteers to share their work. Try for a variety of topics, if appropriate.
- Discuss ways teachers could incorporate differentiation for analytical, practical, and creative thinking in their own classrooms.
- Ask teachers on an exit card: Which type of activity (analytical, practical, or creative) do **you** prefer? Why? Which type do you design most often for your students? Why?

Tips and Differentiation Options

- Change the topics to match the aspects of differentiation you want teachers to focus on. Example (after an introduction to the elements of differentiation):
    - Analytical: Identify the individual components of differentiated instruction. Explain or diagram how these components work together to support varied learner needs.
    - Creative: Brainstorm possible metaphors for differentiated instruction. Choose your best metaphor, and illustrate it with words and/or pictures to help us understand differentiation and see it in a new light.
    - Practical: Based on your own experience, explain how differentiation **can** work in today's classrooms. What are the problems teachers will likely run into as they try to implement differentiation of instruction more fully? How might teachers approach these problems?

    Example (for use after the jigsaw on DI strategies):
    - Analytical: Analyze the similarities and differences among today's strategies for differentiation. Put the results of your analysis into a visual format of your choice (graph or graphic organizer; series of interconnected snapshots, symbols, body poses, etc.) that will help others see both similarities and differences in the strategies. Make sure it is clear **how** or **why** the strategies fit the key principles of the differentiation model.
    - Practical: Rank the strategies in terms of how likely you are to use them in your classroom or staff development plans. Be ready to explain why you ranked them as you did. Now, choose the strategy you are most likely to use, and compose an e-mail or voice mail message that encourages someone

who was not here today to incorporate the strategy into their own teaching or staff development plans. (Consider the characteristics and challenges of your colleague's specific teaching situation, as well as the key principles of good differentiation.)

- Creative: Devise a way to adapt another strategy you are familiar with (or to combine two or more of today's strategies) so that it responds to differences in your students' interests, learning profile, or readiness. Write out the directions for the task. Either within the directions or as a sidebar, annotate your instructions to show how your "invention" fits the key principles of the differentiation model.

- Allow teachers to work alone or with one or two others.
- If your group is large, ask them to share either in same- or mixed-intelligence groups.
- Record the intelligence preference each teacher chose to work in. Use this information for grouping teachers in future staff development sessions.

What to Look For

- Evidence that information is accurate and comprehensive.
- Options no one chose. This may indicate a need for further instruction in or discussion about that aspect of differentiation or further experiences in that intelligence area.

Summarizing the Components of Differentiation

Activity

A colleague sends you an e-mail asking you about one of the following:

- Differentiation in general
- Pre-assessment
- KUD goals
- Respectful activities

You know this colleague's preferred intelligence according to Robert Sternberg's theory, and it happens to match your preference. Select one of the following tasks, and use your knowledge of what appeals to an analytical, practical, or creative learner to design a product that would help your colleague refine his or her understanding of differentiated instruction.

Analytical Task (Choose one.)

Create a flowchart that shows your colleague how to do one of the following. Include where things might go wrong and what to do if they do.

- A. Design a high-quality differentiated lesson.
- B. Design a pre-assessment.
- C. Write an appropriate KUD plan.
- D. Ensure that differentiation is respectful.

Practical Task (Choose one.)

- A. Write a brief vignette or draw and annotate a picture of a student you know whose needs are better met when working in a differentiated classroom.
- B. Role-play about a teacher who learned important things from giving a pre-assessment and what he or she did with the results.
- C. Use your own subject-area expertise to explain the difference between Know, Understand and Do goals.
- D. Give clear examples of the difference between respectful DI and disrespectful DI.

Summarizing the Components of Differentiation

Activity (Cont.)

Creative Task (Choose one.)

Devise an expanded metaphor, a parable, or a short skit that shows your colleague

- A. Why differentiation is important in **all** classrooms (including tracked classes).
- B. The role of pre-assessment in the differentiated classroom.
- C. The difference teaching to the "big idea" or for understanding can make to students.
- D. The difference between respectful differentiation and disrespectful differentiation.

My Task:

Tiered ThinkDots: Reflecting on Differentiation

ACTION TOOL

Rationale and Purpose

There are two versions of this activity. Use Version A with teachers who have some knowledge of the definition, vocabulary, and principles of differentiation. Use Version B with teachers new to differentiation.

Directions

- Before the session:
  - Make copies of whichever version of the ThinkDots prompts you choose to use. You will need one copy for every 3–6 teachers.
  - Working with one sheet at a time, cut the ThinkDots squares apart, punch a hole in the upper left-hand corner of each card, and thread the cards onto a key ring or staple them together at the side.
- Place teachers in groups of 3–6. Distribute one set of cards and a die to each group of teachers.
- Once teachers have completed the activity, discuss the ThinkDots strategy and how they might use it in their own classrooms. Ask teachers:
  - What makes this a good activity? What did you like about it? What concerns do you have?
  - What was the purpose of this activity? What might the KUD goals be?
  - In what way(s) was this activity differentiated? What other ideas for differentiation can you think of?
  - How and where might an activity like this be used in your own classroom?

Tips and Differentiation Options

- Version A works well as a follow-up to a full-day introduction to differentiation.
- Version B works well as an introductory activity to differentiation.
- Use the last discussion question as an exit card to check for practical application.
- Collect the writing exercise (Part 2) to help you evaluate participants' knowledge and understanding of differentiation. Use some of the answers as an introduction to your next session.
- This activity could be made into a cubing activity in which instead of placing each question on a separate card, you place each on one side of a cube. Students then roll the cube instead of the die. Whichever prompt lands face up is the one they answer.
- For ease of use, put versions A and B on different colors of paper.
- If you have a mixed group, group teachers homogeneously according to readiness (background knowledge of differentiation) and distribute Version A or Version B, as appropriate. If you prefer, keep teachers in mixed groups and distribute both versions to each group, but tell teachers to use the set that matches their background when it is their turn to answer.

What to Look For

- Circulate while teachers complete the activity. Jot down particularly insightful thoughts you hear to share in follow-up discussions. Listen also for misconceptions and inaccuracies that need to be addressed.
- Ask teachers for thoughts about how this type of activity could be used in their own classrooms.
- If more than one version of the cube is used, then Part 1 of this activity is differentiated for readiness. It is differentiated for interest in Part 2.

Part Three

Tiered ThinkDots: Reflecting on Differentiation

Version A

Describe It

What vocabulary is associated with differentiated instruction? Define the terms.

Associate It

What child's toy does differentiation remind you of? Explain your thinking.

Apply It

Give an example of how you currently alter your instruction to meet specific learner needs in your classroom. What will you try next?

Analyze It

Think of a question that your students will likely have about differentiated instruction. How will you answer it?

Compare It

Compare differentiated instruction to more "traditional" instruction. Use all of your senses.

Argue For or Against It

Should a school require teachers to differentiate instruction? Explain your reasoning.

Tiered ThinkDots: Reflecting on Differentiation
Version B

Describe It

What are the characteristics of high-quality curriculum?

Associate It

What do you think of when you hear the term "differentiated instruction"?

Apply It

Think about your own experiences in school. What worked well for you? What was difficult?

Analyze It

How is good teaching like your favorite hobby?

Compare It

How does the typical classroom experience of a student who struggles compare with the experience of a student who is advanced?

Argue For or Against It

Classrooms today are so diverse that it is virtually impossible for teachers to meet the needs of their students.

Tiered ThinkDots: Reflecting on Differentiation

Activity

Part 1

- Work in groups of 3–6.
- The first person rolls the die and answers the prompt that corresponds to whatever number lands on top. Work for complete, thoughtful, and even insightful answers.
- Other team members add their own thoughts in response to the prompt.
- The second person rolls the die. If he or she rolls a different number, respond to that prompt; if your group has already answered that prompt, roll again.
- Stop once you have answered all prompts.

Part 2

Working alone, choose any *one* of the prompts.

- Why did you choose this prompt?

- What do you think the KUD goals were for this activity?

- On a separate page, write a brief journal entry in response to the prompt.

References

Arter, J., & McTighe, J. (2001). *Scoring rubrics in the classroom: Using performance criteria for assessing and improving student performance.* Thousand Oaks, CA: Corwin.

Brighton, C. M., Hertberg, H. L., Moon, T. R., Tomlinson, C. A., & Callahan, C. M. (2005). *The feasibility of high-end learning in a diverse middle school.* Storrs, CT: National Research Center on the Gifted and Talented.

Center for Talent Development. (2002). Gifted education in today's schools: An interview with Carolyn Callahan, PhD. Retrieved October 7, 2008, from www.ctd.northwestern.edu/resources/displayArticle/?id=142

Gardner, H. (1991). *The unschooled mind: How children think and how schools should respond.* New York: Basic Books.

Gould, H. C. (2000). Can we meet standards and encourage teachers to differentiate for the highly able? *NASSP Bulletin 84*(614), 74–78.

Guskey. T. R., & Bailey, J. M. (2001). *Developing grading and reporting systems for student learning.* Thousand Oaks, CA: Corwin.

Heacox, D. (2002). *Differentiating instruction in the regular classroom: How to reach and teach all learners, grades 3–12.* Minneapolis, MN: Free Spirit.

Hedrick, K. A. (2005). Staff differentiation must be made to measure. *Journal of Staff Development, 26*(4), 34–37.

Kaufman, H. (1995). *The limits of organizational change.* New Brunswick, NJ: Transaction.

McTighe, J., & Brown, J. (2005). Differentiated instruction and educational standards: Is détente possible? *Theory into Practice, 44*(3), 234–244.

McTighe, J., & Wiggins, G. (2001). *Understanding by Design.* Alexandria, VA: Merrill/Prentice Hall & ASCD.

McTighe, J. & Wiggins, G. (2004). *The Understanding by Design professional development workbook.* Alexandria, VA: ASCD.

O'Connor, K. (2002). *How to grade for learning* (2nd ed.). Thousand Oaks, CA: Corwin.

O'Connor, K. (2007). *A repair kit for grading: 15 fixes for broken grades.* Princeton. NJ: ETS.

Sternberg, R. J., & Grigorenko, E. L. (2007). *Teaching for successful intelligence: To increase student learning and achievement* (2nd ed.). Thousand Oaks, CA: Corwin.

Strickland, C. A. (2007). *Tools for high-quality differentiated instruction:* An ASCD action tool. Alexandria, VA: ASCD.

Tomlinson, C. A. (2000). Reconcilable differences? Standards-based teaching and differentiation. *Educational Leadership, 58*(1), 6–11.

Tomlinson, C. A. (2005, July). PowerPoint presentation at the Summer Institute on Academic Diversity. Charlottesville: Curry School of Education, University of Virginia.

Tomlinson, C. A., & Allan, S. D. (2000). *Leadership for differentiating schools and classrooms.* Alexandria, VA: ASCD.

Tomlinson, C.A., & Eidson, C. C. (2003a). *Differentiation in practice: A resource guide for differentiating curriculum, grades 5–9.* Alexandria, VA: ASCD.

Tomlinson, C.A., & Eidson, C. C. (2003b). *Differentiation in practice: A resource guide for differentiating curriculum, grades K–5.* Alexandria, VA: ASCD.

Tomlinson, C.A., & Strickland, C. A. (2005). *Differentiation in practice: A resource guide for differentiating curriculum, grades 9–12.* Alexandria, VA: ASCD.

Tomlinson, C. A., Kaplan, S. N., Purcell, J. H., Leppein, J. H., Burns, D. E., & Strickland, C. A. (2006). *The parallel curriculum in the classroom, book 2: Units for application across the content areas, K–12.* Thousand Oaks, CA: Corwin.

Wiggins, G., & McTighe, J. (2005). *Understanding by Design* (2nd ed.). Alexandria, VA: ASCD.

Wormeli, R. (2006). *Fair isn't always equal: Assessing & grading in the differentiated classroom.* Portland, ME: Stenhouse.

Wormeli, R. (2007). *Differentiation: From planning to practice, grades 6–12.* Portland, ME: Stenhouse.

About the Author

Cindy A. Strickland has been a teacher for 25 years, working with students from kindergarten to the master's level. As a member of ASCD's Differentiated Instruction Cadre, Strickland works closely with Carol Ann Tomlinson and has coauthored several books and articles with her. In the past eight years, her consulting work has taken her to 46 states, 5 provinces, and 3 continents, where she has conducted workshops on topics relating to differentiation, the Parallel Curriculum Model, and gifted education.

Strickland's ASCD publications on differentiation include *The Professional Learning Community Series: Exploring Differentiated Instruction; Tools for High-Quality Differentiated Instruction*: An ASCD Action Tool (a finalist for 2008 Association of Educational Publishers Distinguished Achievement Award); the ASCD PD Online course *Success with Differentiation*; the book *Differentiation in Practice: A Resource Guide for Differentiating Curriculum, Grades 9–12*; and a unit in the book *Differentiation in Practice: A Resource Guide for Differentiating Curriculum, Grades 5–9*.

Strickland's other publications include *The Parallel Curriculum Model* (2nd edition); *The Parallel Curriculum in the Classroom: Units for Application Across the Content Areas, K–12; Multimedia Kit for the Parallel Curriculum* (a finalist for 2006 Association of Educational Publishers Distinguished Achievement Award); and *In Search of the Dream: Designing Schools and Classrooms That Work for High Potential Students from Diverse Cultural Backgrounds*.

Related ASCD Resources: Differentiated Instruction

At the time of publication, the following ASCD resources were available (ASCD stock numbers appear in parentheses). For up-to-date information about ASCD resources, go to www.ascd.org.

DVDs

At Work in the Differentiated Classroom (three 28- to 48-minute programs on DVD and a 195-page facilitator's guide) (#601071)

Differentiated Instruction in Action (three-disc DVD series) (#608050)

Leadership for Differentiating Instruction (one 100-minute DVD with a comprehensive user guide and bonus DVD features)(#607038)

A Visit to a School Moving Toward Differentiation (one 30-minute DVD with a comprehensive viewer's guide) (#607133)

Mixed Media

Differentiated Instruction in Action (two-disc CD-ROM) (#504031)

Differentiated Instruction Professional Development Planner and Resource Package (Stage 1) (#701225)

Differentiated Instruction Professional Development Planner and Resource Package (Stage 2) (#703402)

Differentiating Instruction for Mixed-Ability Classrooms Professional Inquiry Kit by Carol Ann Tomlinson (#196213)

Online Courses

Differentiated Instruction (#PD00OC09)

Success with Differentiated Instruction (#PD05OC49)

Using Assessment in the Differentiated Classroom (#PD06OC58)

Print Products

The Differentiated Classroom: Responding to the Needs of All Learners by Carol Ann Tomlinson (#199040)

The Differentiated School: Making Revolutionary Changes in Teaching and Learning by Carol Ann Tomlinson, Kay Brimijoin, and Lane Narvaez (#105005)

Fulfilling the Promise of the Differentiated Classroom: Strategies and Tools for Responsive Teaching by Carol Ann Tomlinson (#103107)

How to Differentiate Instruction in Mixed-Ability Classrooms, 2nd edition, by Carol Ann Tomlinson (#101043)

Integrating Differentiated Instruction and Understanding by Design: Connecting Content and Kids by Carol Ann Tomlinson and Jay McTighe (#105004)

Tools for High-Quality Differentiated Instruction by Cindy A. Strickland (#707017)

For more information: send e-mail to member@ascd.org; call 1-800-933-2723 or 703-578-9600, press 2; send a fax to 703-575-5400; or write to Information Services, ASCD, 1703 N. Beauregard St., Alexandria, VA 22311-1714 USA.